Strategy and Compromise

Books by Samuel Eliot Morison

LIFE AND LETTERS OF HARRISON GRAY OTIS, 1913
THE MARITIME HISTORY OF MASSACHUSETTS, 1921
THE OXFORD HISTORY OF THE UNITED STATES, 1927
BUILDERS OF THE BAY COLONY, 1930
THE DEVELOPMENT OF HARVARD UNIVERSITY 1868-1929, 1930
THE FOUNDING OF HARVARD COLLEGE, 1935
HARVARD COLLEGE IN THE SEVENTEENTH CENTURY, 1936
THREE CENTURIES OF HARVARD, 1936
THE SECOND VOYAGE OF COLUMBUS, 1939
ADMIRAL OF THE OCEAN SEA: A LIFE OF CHRISTOPHER COLUMBUS, 1942
THE ROPEMAKERS OF PLYMOUTH, 1950
BY LAND AND BY SEA, 1953
HISTORY OF UNITED STATES NAVAL OPERATIONS IN WORLD WAR II

    I   THE BATTLE OF THE ATLANTIC, 1947
    II   OPERATIONS IN NORTH AFRICAN WATERS, 1947
    III   THE RISING SUN IN THE PACIFIC, 1948
    IV   CORAL SEA, MIDWAY, AND SUBMARINE ACTIONS, 1949
    V   THE STRUGGLE FOR GUADALCANAL, 1949
    VI   BREAKING THE BISMARCKS BARRIER, 1950
    VII   ALEUTIANS, GILBERTS AND MARSHALLS, 1951
    VIII   NEW GUINEA AND THE MARIANAS, 1953
    IX   SICILY — SALERNO — ANZIO, 1954
    X   THE ATLANTIC BATTLE WON, 1956
    XI   THE INVASION OF FRANCE AND GERMANY, 1957

CHRISTOPHER COLUMBUS, MARINER, 1955
THE INTELLECTUAL LIFE OF COLONIAL NEW ENGLAND, 1956. (The first edition, 1936, was called THE PURITAN PRONAOS.)
FREEDOM IN CONTEMPORARY SOCIETY, 1956
STRATEGY AND COMPROMISE, 1958

(With Henry Steele Commager)
THE GROWTH OF THE AMERICAN REPUBLIC. Fourth edition, 1950

(Editor)
OF PLYMOUTH PLANTATION, by William Bradford, 1952
THE PARKMAN READER, 1955

SAMUEL ELIOT MORISON

STRATEGY
AND
COMPROMISE

An Atlantic Monthly Press Book

BOSTON • Little, Brown and Company • TORONTO

Preface

The nucleus of this little book was a lecture on *American Naval Strategy in World War II* delivered at Phillips Exeter Academy in February, 1957. The substance of it was given in two lectures on *American Contributions to the Strategy of World War II* at the University of Oxford in May. During the summer I revised and enlarged these for publication.

Among the authors and books to whom I am indebted both for ideas and information are Kent Roberts Greenfield *The Historian and the Army*; Matloff and Snell *Strategic Planning for Coalition Warfare*, two volumes in the official *U.S. Army in World War II series*; John Ehrman's two volumes on *Grand Strategy* in the British official *History of the Second World War* edited by J. R. M. Butler; Sir Winston Churchill *The Second World War*, especially Volumes V and VI; Walter Bedell Smith *Eisenhower's Six Great Decisions*; Sir Arthur Bryant *The*

Turn of the Tide, without whose provocation this book would be less interesting than I hope it is; and Captain B. H. Liddell Hart, whose many books on Strategy are excellent, but whose conversation is even better.

The eleven completed volumes of my *History of United States Naval Operations in World War II*, and Volume XII, *Leyte*, which I am now preparing, may be consulted by the reader who wants more details on strategy, or would like to follow the tactical story of the naval war. Captain Bern Anderson USN, my principal assistant in this work, has also been my teacher in strategy.

In putting together a book of this sort one has to fight the tendency to illustrate principles with too many details, thus obscuring rather than developing the points that one is trying to make. Herein my beloved wife, Priscilla B. Morison, has been of the greatest assistance; for not only has she listened critically to the lectures and the text, but also she has been astute in detecting anything that might seem illogical to the expert or confusing to the reader.

SAMUEL ELIOT MORISON

"Good Hope"
Northeast Harbor, Maine
1 September 1957

Contents

CONTENTS

I

The War in Europe

I

Strategy, Higher Strategy, and Tactics

American contributions to the strategy of World
War II may roughly be summarized as follows:

First, the American share in the major strategic
decision of March 1941, which remained in force
until victory was won.

Second, American contributions to the strategy of
the European theater, especially to the invasion of
the Continent.

Third, the strategy of the war against Japan in the
Pacific, which was almost completely American.

In the European theater British and American conceptions of the proper strategy for the defeat of the
European Axis differed widely, and the course actually followed was a compromise between the two.
In the Pacific, however, the British were generally
disposed to give the United States a free hand, and
the strategy of the war with Japan issued from the

Joint Chiefs of Staff, although initiated by the staffs of Admirals King and Nimitz and General Mac-Arthur.

Before we get into the subject, a few definitions are in order. Strategy is well defined in the *Concise Oxford Dictionary* as "the art of so moving or disposing troops or ships" — to which we must now add "aircraft" — "as to impose upon the enemy the place and time and conditions for fighting preferred by oneself"; and to this I would add, "the art of defeating the enemy in the most economical and expeditious manner." Strategy is distinct from tactics, which means the moving of military, naval and air forces in "actual contact with the enemy." In other words, tactics start where strategy ends, but both are the means of carrying a war to a successful conclusion. For instance, General Lee's decision to cross the Potomac into Maryland in 1862 was strategy, but the manner in which he fought General McClellan at Antietam was tactics. The British decision in 1942 to hang on in the desert west of Egypt was a matter of strategy; whilst General Montgomery's directives for the Battle of El Alamein, and the execution thereof, were tactical.

Bad strategy can render the most brilliant tactics

4

fruitless, as happened many times in the American Civil War. Conversely, sound tactics are necessary to implement good strategy. For instance, the concept of the Gallipoli Campaign in World War I may be defended as sound strategy, but the Allied tactics were so haphazard and ineffective as to make that campaign a dismal failure. In World War II, the plan for defeating Germany by first invading France over the Normandy beaches was strategy; while the way it was done — whether the troops should land at night or by day, and at what stage of the tide; how the air forces should be employed, and how much naval bombardment should be hurled at the target before the troops landed — was tactics. In the Pacific it was the American air strategy to tangle with the Japanese Air Force at every opportunity in order to wear it down; and the famous Thach Weave (two columns of fighter planes crisscrossing in attack) was one of the tactics that wore it down so successfully that in one year Japan built ten thousand planes and lost 70 per cent of them.

We must also keep clear the distinction between military strategy, with which I am here concerned, and grand or higher strategy, whose function Captain Liddell Hart has defined as "to coördinate and direct all the resources of a nation towards the attainment of the political object of the war — the goal defined by national policy. Whereas strategy is only concerned with the problem of winning military victory, grand strategy must take the longer view — for its problem in the winning of the peace." [1] This grand or higher strategy is simply national foreign policy continued in time of war. The British Commonwealth and the United States throughout this century have consistently been striving (though often with inadequate means and inconsistent methods) for a stable and peaceful world in which they can "do business" in other ways than at the point of a gun. Even the Spanish American War of 1898 and the South African War of 1899-1901 fall into this category, as do the various British "punitive expeditions" on the Indian frontier, the last wars of the United States against the Red Indians, and the American interventions in Mexico, Haiti, Nicaragua and the Dominican Republic. In World War I the famous "Fourteen Points," in World War II the "Atlantic Charter," were acts of higher strategy, as was the "Unconditional Surrender" pronouncement

[1] B. H. Liddell Hart "The Objective in War" (a lecture delivered to the U.S. Naval War College, 24 Sept. 1952) p. 25, and his book *Strategy* (New York, 1954) pp. 335-336, 362.

made by the Western Allies, almost heedlessly and without counting the consequences, in January 1943. Whilst political considerations should have no place in military strategy (but often, alas, do, in numerous instances of incompetent commanders being protected by political pressure), political considerations should have a more important weight in higher or grand strategy than, of late, they generally have had. In World War II the Western Allies lost sight of the old principle that our enemies of today may be wanted as allies of tomorrow. We beat down Japan and Germany so severely that we have had to pay heavily to rebuild their military power for the so-called Cold War, a relatively bloodless war on a planetary scale, played for no less stakes than the whole of Eastern Asia, the Middle East and Africa.

7

2

Mistakes in Strategy

In warfare, mistakes are inevitable. Military decisions are based on estimates of the enemy's strength and intentions that are usually faulty, and on Intelligence that is never complete and is often misleading. Tactical errors by a general in the field, a group commander in the air or an officer in tactical command of a naval task force are frequent, because they are necessarily based on an almost instantaneous appreciation of a fluid, constantly changing situation. Strategical errors are less common in modern warfare. Every important command, as well as the chiefs of staff, has a group of planners selected for their knowledge and intelligence, who make long-range plans based not only on an estimate of the enemy's intentions and capabilities, but on a thorough knowledge of one's own strength and capabilities, including logistics. Nevertheless, mistakes in strategy are made; and it may be said that, other things being equal, the side that makes the fewer strategic errors wins the war.

It is very easy for a writer on military history to get a hearing for the thesis that his own country's strategy was bad. The British and American public like to be told that their leaders were stupid and made horrible mistakes, which some clever New York journalist or a Labour M.P. pointed out at the time. But it is very difficult to prove that these alleged strategic errors really were errors. Almost everyone who argues that a strategic decision in Allied strategy during World War II was wrong assumes that if we had done something different the enemy would still have done the same thing that he actually did. That, in most cases, is a major fallacy; for, if we had done something different, the enemy would have altered his strategy to counteract it. I can think, however, of one instance in World War II where a strategic mistake by us can be proved, because if we had done the different thing, the enemy had no means of meeting it. I refer to Operation TORCH, in which the British and United States Navy concept was undoubtedly better than the American Army concept of dividing the landings between Casablanca, Oran and Algiers. If we had "nipped into Bizerta," as Admiral Sir Andrew Cunningham put it, we could have secured Tunisia promptly and saved both time and precious lives.

In higher strategy it is easier to detect and nail errors than in ordinary military strategy, because cause and effect can often be accurately assessed. It was, for instance, a major error of British higher strategy to insist on parity between the British and American Navies in 1919 and the years following. Any child can now see that there was no possible danger of a third Anglo-American war, and every reason for Britain to support America in building up the world's strongest navy. At the same time American higher strategy made two major errors: (1) insisting on the termination of the Anglo-Japanese treaty alliance concluded twenty years earlier, and (2) confronting the Japanese with the 5-5-3 naval formula. The one act caused the Japanese to feel that they were being pushed outside the family of civilized nations, and the latter gave their militarists a wonderful lever to stir up popular animosity against the Anglo-American powers.

It may also be argued that the entire range of American higher strategy in the Orient during this century, the ultimate purpose of which was to maintain the integrity and independence of China, was a

mistake; since, after a long and bloody war to implement this policy, the end product was the establish-
ment of Red China. Nevertheless, the alternative, a
China controlled by Japanese militarists, might have
been even worse. Almost everyone admits that the
Anglo-French higher strategy of appeasing Hitler
by acquiescing in his occupation of the Rhineland,
annexation of Austria and rape of Czechoslovakia
was a mistake, since it encouraged him to strike for
higher stakes; and he had to be fought, after all —
without the aid of the Czech army. And I will freely
admit that the isolationist policy of the United States
between the two world wars was a grave mistake.

It is also abundantly clear that the Anglo-American coalition was mistaken in its higher strategy during the war toward Russia. That policy was based on
two assumptions, both of which can now be proved
false: (1) that there was grave danger that Stalin,
if not sufficiently supported with matériel and ap-
peased by political concessions, would conclude a
separate peace with Germany, as Lenin had done in
1917, and leave the Western Allies holding the bag.
(2) That if we treated Russia honorably and gen-
erously, Communist hostility to us would be as-
suaged and Russia would continue to be a dependa-

ble ally after victory was achieved. We now know that there was no chance — except in the case of an overwhelming German victory — of the U.S.S.R. concluding a separate peace; and we have bitterly learned that the long-range higher strategy of Communism, its determination to subvert and destroy all governments not dominated by Reds, was only temporarily suspended during the war.

A few more definitions before we get at the basic strategy of World War II. The Joint Chiefs of Staff, to whom I shall frequently refer, were the heads of the United States Army, Navy and Army Air Force. Throughout the war these were General George C. Marshall, Chief of Staff of the Army; Admiral Ernest J. King, Chief of Naval Operations; and General H. H. ("Hap") Arnold, the head of the Army Air Force — with Admiral Leahy, Chief of Staff to President Roosevelt, the Commander in Chief, as Chairman. The British Chiefs of Staff (more properly called the Committee of the British Chiefs of Staff), were Field Marshal Sir Alan Brooke (now Lord Alanbrooke), Chief of the Imperial General Staff (C.I.G.S.); the First Sea Lord (Admiral Sir Dudley Pound, succeeded by Admiral Lord Cunningham); and Air Chief Marshal Sir Charles Portal (now Lord

Portal). These two bodies together, the Joint Chiefs of Staff and the British Chiefs of Staff, formed the *Combined Chiefs of Staff* who determined the strategy of the war, subject to the approval of the President and of the Prime Minister. Roosevelt and Churchill met with the C.C.S. in several plenary conferences during the war, at Washington, Casablanca, Quebec, Cairo, and Yalta; and Stalin joined them at Teheran; but Russia seldom, if ever, informed the Western Allies as to her intentions, and took no interest in their strategy, other than to exert pressure on them to establish a Second Front in Europe at the earliest possible moment.

Mr. Churchill, as Minister of Defence, did not have the same constitutional supremacy over his Chiefs of Staff as Roosevelt did over the J.C.S., because in Britain the King, not the Minister of Defence, is Commander in Chief of the nation's armed forces. Nevertheless, Mr. Churchill had far more influence over the B.C.S. than did Mr. Roosevelt over the J.C.S. This came about partly because Churchill met with the British Chiefs of Staff very frequently and kept them up most of the night arguing with them; and partly because, having been a soldier himself and First Lord of the Admiralty in World

13

War I, he thought he knew as much or more about strategy than they did. President Roosevelt had a very modest opinion of his own military knowledge compared with the "Former Naval Person" who corresponded with him so intimately. F.D.R. seldom met the Joint Chiefs of Staff and was much more amenable to military counsel than the Prime Minister was to his generals, admirals and air marshals. The President, like the Prime Minister, was apt to entertain extravagant strategical ideas; but, unlike the Prime Minister, he could usually be kept on the straight-and-narrow path by General Marshall and Admirals King and Leahy. As Lord Alanbrooke has recently (and indiscreetly) revealed, Mr. Churchill was often very difficult to dissuade from some favorite objective like Operation JUPITER for the invasion of Norway. Sir Arthur Bryant gives us to understand that it was Field Marshal Brooke who won over the Prime Minister to sound views; but I believe that he claims too much for his subject in this as in other respects. Field Marshal Smuts, Admiral Pound and Air Chief Marshal Portal were also powerful dissuaders in their own way. But there were also occasions when the only way that the British Chiefs of Staff could get out of something that the P.M. in-

sisted upon was to signal Field Marshal Sir John
Dill, their representative in Washington, to see General Marshall and beg him to induce the President to
persuade Churchill that what he insisted on being
done simply could not be done. Conversely, when
the Combined Chiefs of Staff made a decision that
Mr. Churchill did not like, he sometimes tried to
work on Mr. Roosevelt to have it overthrown. A
strange way to handle the strategy of a war, indeed!
But it seemed to work. It could never have worked
except for the close, almost brotherly relations established between Dill, who had the very highest wis-
dom and tact, and Marshall, who recalls George
Washington for integrity of character and complete
honesty. Nor could it have worked without a chief of
state endowed with the high political sense, and the
capacity to distinguish good advice from bad, that
characterized Franklin D. Roosevelt; or, let me add,
a war leader with the energy, the inspiring leader-
ship, and the capacity (after endless argument) to
yield to good advice that characterized Winston
Churchill.

This is, I admit, a very different explanation of the
way that our strategy in Europe was worked out
from the simple one of Sir Arthur Bryant that it all

issued from the massive brain of Field Marshal Sir Alan Brooke. Bryant would have us believe that every American in a position to influence strategy was an amiable amateur in the act of war, who had never commanded any great number of troops or worked on strategical problems. But General Marshall had been a planning officer on General Pershing's staff in 1918, Admiral Stark had been flag secretary to Admiral Sims from November 1917 to the end of that war, Admiral King had been assistant chief of staff to Admiral Mayo, Commander in Chief Atlantic Fleet in World War I; and General Eisenhower, before he was called to high command, had been chief of the war plans division of the War Department. These, and the planning officers like Captain Forrest Sherman and General Wedemeyer who worked on committees of the J.C.S., had taken courses on strategy at our war colleges since World War I and had thought deeply on strategy. The two admirals on the J.C.S., King and Leahy, had pronounced views on military and air as well as naval strategy; and the fact that they and Marshall often disagreed with Brooke does not necessarily prove that they were wanting in strategical knowledge or common sense.

3

Basic Strategic Decisions

Let us now take up the basic American ideas on the strategy of the war. World War I had been embarked upon by the United States before she was in any way prepared to fight, and with no definite high strategy, or strategic plan — not even the machinery for co-operating with England and France. As a consequence, in that war, America depended on British shipping to get her troops across, on the French 75's to arm her artillery; and even on the Royal Air Force for aircraft. President Roosevelt and his military advisors were determined not to let this happen again. At his urging, Congress began building up the United States Navy to treaty limits in 1938. The question of what strategy we would follow if a second world war broke out was an object of study by the Joint Planning Committee of the United States armed forces the same year. In April 1939, five months before the war started in Europe, the Joint Board, predecessors of the Joint Chiefs of Staff, issued a secret report to the Chief of Staff that in the event of a war with Germany, Italy, and Japan, the European Axis should be defeated first.[2]

World War II broke out in September 1939. After a winter of the so-called "phony war" where each side warily watched the other, Germany beat France to her knees, gained control of the entire coastline of the Continent from Norway to Spain, and, in conjunction with Mussolini's Italy, became almost overnight the dominant power in the Mediterranean. In September 1940, the big German air bombing attack on England opened. These events made American intervention in the European war, in order to save Western civilization, almost a certainty.

This statement requires explanation. American isolationism was still so strong in 1939 that advocates of our intervention on the side of England and France hardly dared to speak, and leaders like President Roosevelt could only persuade Congress to vote for increased armaments by talking in terms of national

---

[2] Louis Morton in *Military Review* (December 1949). This Report included the prophetic statement that "a probable Japanese measure would be to damage major fleet units without warning, or possibly attempt to block the Fleet in Pearl Harbor."

defense, inter-American neutrality patrol, and the like. The traditional prejudice against balance-of-power concepts was also strong. Sympathy with England and France, and a feeling of loathing for Fascism and the Nazis was also strong; but it was generally believed here — as also in England and France — that the Axis could be defeated without American aid. The Axis victories of 1940 changed all that. The hegemony that Germany and Italy had won, almost overnight, over Continental Europe, drove home to thinking Americans that the balance of power must be redressed. They realized that if England fell, America as a nation would be in grave peril; that if Germany gained control of Northwest Africa, South America would be within her orbit; that the Atlantic was no longer a barrier, but a bridge.

The big "if" that American strategic thinkers discussed was, whether in the event that we did get involved in a war with Germany, we would not have to fight Japan as well. And if we did, what were we going to do about it? Admiral Harold R. Stark, Chief of Naval Operations, in a memorandum that he laid on the desk of the Secretary of the Navy in November 1940, recommended that if we became involved in a two-ocean war, we should start with offensive strategy in Europe, and a defensive one in the Pacific. General Marshall agreed, and so did the President and his three principal Secretaries. In 1940 the first "Two-ocean Navy" Acts were passed, the National Guard was called into active service, the military draft was passed by Congress, and the Lend-Lease Acts, ignoring the old juridical conception of neutrality, definitely arrayed the United States on the side of the British Commonwealth.

In these preparations the most important single event for future strategy, and one which proved how far the American armed forces were ready to co-operate, was the Combined Staff Conference in Washington during February and March 1941, nine months before the United States formally entered the war. This secret conference between Army, Navy and Air Force representatives of both nations included some of their best brains, such as Captain Alan G. Kirk and Rear Admiral Richmond Kelly Turner USN, Major General S. D. Embick USA, Rear Admiral Roger Bellairs and V. H. Dankwerts RN, Major General E. L. Morris and Air Vice Marshal John Slessor. After prolonged discussions the ABC-1 Staff agreement of 27 March 1941 was drafted.

This provided that, *if and when* America entered the war, her principal military effort would be exerted in the European theater; that she would try to avoid war with Japan; but that even if Japan attacked the United States, operations in the Pacific would be conducted in such manner as to facilitate the effort against Germany. Although the last clause was rather "woolly" — since how could one fight in the Pacific in such manner as to help the war in Europe? — the meaning was plain: "Beat Hitler first."

So important a decision needs some explanation. What reasons impelled these American strategists to agree with their British fellows to beat Hitler first? (1) Because Germany had a greater military potential than Japan, and it was feared she might uncork some secret weapon of devastating power if given time — a fear realized in the V-1 and V-2 guided bombs and rockets. (2) Because Germany already had control of the entire western coast of Europe, excepting Spain and Portugal, and so threatened the sea communications of North and South America. (3) England was already engaged in fighting Germany, and could be assisted in that fight immediately; whilst Japan, in March 1941, was fighting only

China, and it would be very difficult to get aid to China.

Hence, the leaders of the Armed Forces of the United States decided in March 1941 that if and when we were involved in the war, even in a war on two oceans, we would put forth our first and best efforts to the defeat of Germany. That was the major overall strategy of the war. It became the more obvious and pressing when Hitler attacked Russia in June 1941; for if Germany defeated Russia and obtained control of her manpower and resources, he would become almost irresistible. The United States Government remained steadfastly loyal to the decision, despite irritation with British reluctance to strike at Hitler's throat in 1942, and the pressure of a powerful newspaper and die-hard isolationists to concentrate on fighting Japan. For one of the curious traits of the American isolationist is that his fancied island has only one coast, on the Atlantic; a trans-Pacific war seems to have no terrors for him.

4

Opposing Concepts for Defeating Germany

In August 1941 President Roosevelt met Mr. Churchill on board a British battleship in the harbor of Argentia, Newfoundland. By that time Congress had authorized and the President had directed sundry measures "short of war" against Germany. These measures were designed to protect our lifeline to England and the matériel that we were sending her under Lend-Lease. With the reluctant and tardy consent of Iceland, we had relieved the British as an occupying force in that strategically placed island, both to prevent the Germans from taking it, and to use it as an air and naval base. At the Argentia Conference the British Chiefs of Staff unveiled their views on the proper strategy to beat the European Axis. These were: (1) to maintain a tight naval blockade of the Axis countries; (2) intensive air bombing of key points in Germany; (3) propaganda and assistance to resistance groups in all occupied countries; (4) "closing and tightening the ring" about Germany, thrusting armored forces in amphibious landings all around the Axis periphery; and, finally, (5) a full-powered strike into Germany itself, after Hitler's Reich had been so weakened that the invasion would be a pushover.

This strategy was viewed by the American Joint Chiefs of Staff, especially by General Marshall and Admiral King, with dismay. They agreed that a tight blockade must be maintained, and that the sea lanes must be kept open. Our top air force general, "Hap" Arnold, had confidence that prolonged heavy bombing would break down German morale and destroy munitions factories. But nobody could figure out how a succession of "hit and run" raids around the ring of Hitler's *Festung Europa* could bring victory any nearer. To us this seemed a strategy of weakness: something to be done to keep your spirits up when you could do nothing better. The American idea was to begin immediate planning and preparing for a massive assault aimed at the heart of Germany. This, incidentally, had been the American strategy in World War I, at a time when many British leaders preferred to get at Germany by some "back door."

A large part of the strategic discussion about the European theater between the Americans and British, between the Joint Chiefs of Staff and the British Chiefs of Staff, was between those two conceptions — the massive thrust at the enemy's heart, and successive stabs around the periphery to bleed the enemy to death, like jackals worrying a lion before springing at his throat. From the time America entered the war, the Joint Chiefs of Staff worked for sixteen months before they could obtain the consent of their British opposite numbers to set up the cross-Channel assault that finally took place, very successfully, in 1944, and whose direct consequence was the defeat of Germany. In order to persuade the British Chiefs of Staff to agree to this, the United States had to take part more or less unwillingly in a series of Mediterranean campaigns and to stand idly by while the British wasted their manpower and Canada's on hit-and-run raids such as those on St. Nazaire and Dieppe, and on the extraneous and unnecessary assault on Diego Suarez.

There were, however, excellent reasons for the British attitude, as the Americans soon learned. (1) Britain was almost completely mobilized for war by the time the United States entered it, and could not raise many more troops; but she had a very powerful Navy and merchant marine. It therefore seemed the best employment for her armed forces to use the Navy to escort and lift such forces as she had to make hit-and-run raids. And, in the meantime, the Allies would be growing stronger and Germany weaker. (2) Britain had a strong tradition of "desultory and haphazard operations" — to use the phrase of an American naval historian about her raids during our War of Independence. Sir Winston Churchill himself wrote, in one of the recent instalments of his *History of Great Britain*, "With an imprudence which is difficult to understand . . . outposts from the British Army in New York were flung about in careless fashion through the New Jersey towns, and Washington determined to strike at these isolated bodies before General Howe could cross the Delaware" — which Washington did, to very good purpose, at Trenton, Princeton and elsewhere.[3] Other examples are the descents on the Dutch coast, Cadiz and the Ile de Rhé in the seventeenth century, and the landings on the Dutch coast and at Quiberon Bay in 1795. Britain had got at Napoleon by the back door through Spain; and Mr. Churchill always felt

---

[3] *Life* Magazine (15 April 1957).

that his Gallipoli strategy in World War I, if implemented by proper tactics, could have defeated Germany by way of her "soft underbelly." On the other hand, in the one modern war in which England attempted to make a massive direct attack on a Continental enemy, she had suffered terribly. The British Empire lost almost a million men in France in 1914-1918.[4] Every Englishman in a responsible position was determined to avoid another frightful, useless bloodletting. On one occasion when General Marshall was in England, pouring forth the most cogent and logical arguments in favor of a prompt invasion of the Continent, a distinguished civilian, the late Lord Cherwell, remarked to him, "It's no use — you are arguing against the casualties on the Somme." Moreover, in World War I, England and the United States could land their troops easily at docksides in an Allied country, but this time they would have to fight their way in across a wall of steel and concrete, bristling with guns. These were the main reasons for the British strategy of probe, jab,

---

[4] I know of no more eloquent memorial than the simple inscription on a tablet erected by the British Government in Notre Dame de Paris: TO THE GLORY OF GOD AND TO THE MEMORY OF ONE MILLION MEN OF THE BRITISH EMPIRE WHO FELL IN THE GREAT WAR, 1914-1918, AND OF WHOM THE GREATER PART REST IN FRANCE.

bomb, subvert; followed by the final big push when an opening occurred, or when Germany seemed ready to crack. But if the United States had accepted this strategy, and not pressed for something more vigorous, Germany could hardly have been defeated before 1946, if then. The elephant doesn't like mice, but a thousand mice can't kill an elephant.

It should be said that not all British strategists were as peripheral-minded as Mr. Churchill. General Sir Frederick Morgan, for instance, as soon as he studied the problem, wished to concentrate on the cross-Channel thrust. Sir Arthur Bryant, in his recent *The Turn of the Tide*, claims for his hero a strategy of concentration, but on the enemy's southern, not his northern and western flanks. Sir Alan Brooke, quite early in the war, wished to combine successive jabs in the Mediterranean into a pattern of ascending steps towards Southern Germany: Morocco, Algeria, Tunisia, Sicily, Salerno, and up the boot of Italy. But, from the record of Brooke's own diary, it is clear that he opposed the first steps of Operation TORCH for the invasion of Africa; that he feared, in June 1942, lest the Prime Minister and F.D.R. would cook it up — as they were actually doing. If anyone is to be considered the Scipio Africanus of World War II he

should be Sir Winston Churchill, with Mr. Roosevelt
as an enthusiastic supporter. They put over TORCH
against the wishes of most of their military advisors,
and upon it Brooke built his later concept of the
ascending Mediterranean ladder. Brooke's strategy
certainly made sense; but the Joint Chiefs of Staff
did not want a piece of it, since they figured out that
it would consume more of our forces than of the
enemy's, and delay the cross-Channel operation at
least a year — as indeed it did.

With these opposed strategic concepts, it was a
wonder that we ever did agree. When Mr. Churchill
proposed a peripheral landing, anywhere between
Norway and Dakar, Mr. Roosevelt was apt to re-
tort, "All right, but where do we go from there?"
which vexed the Prime Minister, since from many
of his favorite targets you could not go anywhere.
On the other hand, the American strategists, especially Generals Marshall and Eisenhower, irritated
their opposite numbers by their cheery optimism; an
apparent belief that if we once got a beachhead on
the Continent we could go right on. British soldiers
freshly remembered the beachheads in Norway,
France and Greece from which they had been ex-
pelled by the Germans in 1940-1941. They had no

intention of running the risk of a second Dunkirk, or of an Athenian Syracusan expedition. The American promises of war production, in 1942, seemed to the British oversanguine, even fantastic, although in the end the reality far surpassed the promise. Sir Arthur Bryant and Lord Alanbrooke represent General Marshall as being a charming man, but an amateur in strategy. They tell a story of his having no ideas whatsoever about troop deployment after landing in France. General Marshall has adopted a policy of dignified silence about these war controversies, so I cannot quote him; but I am confident that his strategic ideas did not stop at the water-edge; that he had a very definite concept of land strategy — namely, the double envelopment of the Ruhr which was actually carried out in 1945 against the strong objections of Field Marshals Brooke and Montgomery.

5

German Submarine and Allied Antisubmarine Strategy

It is almost correct to say that Hitler had no naval strategy. He was *landsinnig*, land-minded; he thought he could rule the waves by conquering the land, taking on the nations that stood in his way one by one. He made the same mistakes as did Napoleon. One must be struck by the parallel — Hitler's ill-conceived plans and violent threats to invade England; his rash attack on Russia in 1941 like Napoleon's in 1812 — and for the same reason: to bring Russia within his Continental system; his reliance on what naval strategists call *la guerre de course*, which in this case took the form of submarine warfare, as Napoleon's took the form of commerce-destroying by privateers.

Hitler left naval strategy largely to Grossadmiral Doenitz, whose one idea was to sink as many Allied ships as possible, disrupt Allied sea communications, and prevent American help from reaching Europe. This policy was based on Doenitz's "integral tonnage" concept — namely, that the job of the U-boats was to sink Allied and neutral tonnage, without regard to the vessel's route or the nature of her cargo, faster than the Allies could replace losses by new construction. He was very flexible and clever in concentrating on unprotected shipping lanes — for instance, against the East Coast of the United States in early 1942 — and then pulling off his wolf-packs as soon as we developed effective escort-of-convoy and countermeasures. Despite all the destruction he wrought, the curve of Allied replacement shipping passed that of shipping losses late in 1942, and went up and up; and the Allies developed their antisubmarine measures to such good purpose that Doenitz, who in February 1942 sank forty-two ships for each U-boat lost, in May 1944 sank only four ships, while losing forty-one of his U-boats.

Fortunately there was no conflict between the American and the British Chiefs of Staff as to the strategy to be used against U-boats. The agreed strategy may be described as escort-of-convoy by ships and aircraft, and the development of special devices to outwit the Germans. Admiral King has been accused by Captain Stephen Roskill RN, in Volume I of his *The War at Sea*, of coolness towards the convoy; but that is not correct. King was slow to organize convoys along the Atlantic coast of the United States simply because he had not the means; the United States Navy had not anticipated the need for corvettes and other small, fast escort vessels. King was steeped in the tradition of Admiral Sims, who had induced the Admiralty to organize convoys in the dark days of 1917. To General Marshall he wrote in 1942, "The convoy is not only *a* way to protect shipping, it is the *only* way." He and Admiral Ingersoll, Commander in Chief of the Atlantic Fleet, were protagonists of the roving hunter-killer groups built around escort carriers which operated in wide support of convoys, relentlessly hunting down every U-boat that approached within two or three hundred miles of a convoy. Doenitz unwittingly helped this strategy by keeping his wolf-packs under tight tactical control through radio; this enabled our high-frequency direction finders to spot the location of his boats, to hunt them down, and to route convoys evasively. But these were tactics, not strategy, as was the important decision made at Washington in April

1943 to let the British and Royal Canadian Navies protect the northern transatlantic route while the United States Navy took care of the central transatlantic route, New York and West Indies to Gibraltar, and the north-south routes between Boston and Brazil. The Royal Navy had always protected the north-south routes on the eastern side of the Atlantic, and continued to do so.

As Allied antisubmarine surface and air forces increased, Doenitz was forced to send his U-boats further and further afield in search of game. After mid-1944, the only area where they had any success was the Indian Ocean, over which the Allies were unable as yet to escort their shipping. At the very end of the war he obtained some sudden success in the North Atlantic and the English Channel with his new snorkel-equipped submarines. But the real test of his strategy, and of our counterstrategy, was the great invasion of Normandy. Our two navies, combat and merchant, lifted some 1,500,000 American troops to England without losing a man to U-boat attack;[5] and the massive invasion of France

[5] By the end of the war there were 2,600,000 American troops (including those of the A.A.F.) on the European Continent, and these figures do not include troops in the Mediterranean theater. But after D-day, most of the American reinforcements were lifted directly to France.

was not troubled by a single U-boat until it had been going on for two weeks. Even thereafter, the attacks on cross-Channel convoys by enemy submarines were sporadic and the losses acceptable.

Let us now return to the major strategy for the invasion of the Continent.

6

The Invasion of France and the Italian Campaign

In the early spring of 1942, the Joint Staff Planners in Washington, a group which included Generals Eisenhower and Wedemeyer and Captain Forrest Sherman USN, prepared a plan for invading the Continent in 1942 and in 1943. We may call it "the Marshall plan," as the Chief of Staff of the Army got strongly behind it, as did Mr. Stimson, the Secretary of War, and, with somewhat less enthusiasm, Admiral King. Germany had declared war on the United States in December 1941, immediately after Pearl Harbor, and her underwater fleet had pulled off a very costly blitz along our East Coast. But by April 1942, except for the British campaign against Rommel in North Africa, the Allies were not fighting German troops anywhere. Russia was doing 95

per cent of the land fighting, and Russia was halloo-
ing very loudly for help. We were sending what
help we could, in munitions and matériel — by the
long Persian Gulf route and the costly Murmansk
route, where Convoy PQ-17 lost twenty-two out of
thirty-three of its merchant ships and 65 per cent of
their cargoes — but Russia demanded a "Second
Front, Now" and all her friends in Britain and the
United States took up the cry.

This Marshall plan was no sinister scheme to help
the Reds. It was simply a practical plan to build up
American armed forces in Britain rapidly, and give
tanks, landing craft and LSTs highest priority in
production, so that we could establish a beachhead
in France in August or September 1942, and pull
off the big invasion in 1943. We started sending
American troops to the United Kingdom as early as
January 1942; and in April, when it seemed likely
that the British would go along with our plan, we
gave triple-A (top) priority to the building of landing and beaching craft, much to the detriment of the
destroyer escort and escort carrier programs. (The
statement in Sir Arthur Bryant's book that landing
craft were only twentieth on our list that summer
is contrary to fact.) But production schedules, troop

training and troop lift to Britain could not be worked out until the British Chiefs of Staff agreed on a date for the invasion.

The British Chiefs of Staff, after an initial acceptance of the Marshall plan as a basis for planning, rejected it, cold. The concept called for a limited beachhead in France in 1942 — Operation SLEDGE-HAMMER — and the big drive, ROUNDUP, in 1943. The B.C.S. had no faith in American ability to prepare for these operations in time; they insisted that Germany would still be too strong; we must continue to lunge around the ring and hope for the best. Marshall, King and Roosevelt argued in vain; and as the United States could not go ahead with the 1942-1943 invasion if England played the reluctant dragon, it had to be given up.

General Marshall told me last year that the great lesson he learned in 1942 was this: in wartime the politicians have to do *something* important every year. They could not simply use 1942 to build up for 1943 or 1944; they could not face the obloquy of fighting another "phony war." The "something" promoted by Mr. Churchill and accepted by President Roosevelt, against the wishes of his military advisors, was Operation TORCH, the invasion of North

Africa. Admirals King and Leahy would have preferred to have redeployed our forces into the Pacific, and to have pursued the war primarily against Japan rather than wait a year or two for the British Chiefs of Staff to make up their minds to lay on a cross-Channel invasion. But President Roosevelt put a veto on that. He felt that we were committed to the "beat Germany first" decision, even if the British insisted on delay; and his historic memories of our old war with the Barbary Corsairs, as well as his inherent romanticism, made him predisposed to the African adventure.

So, the invasion of North Africa was substituted for SLEDGEHAMMER and became our one campaign in the European theater for 1942. When TORCH was set up in June 1942 for execution in November, Roosevelt and Churchill still nourished the delusion that they could have their strategic cake and eat it too; that they could invade North Africa that year, and set up ROUNDUP, the big-cross-Channel operation, for the summer of 1943. Admiral King and General Marshall, more realistic, predicted that TORCH would kill ROUNDUP, as indeed it did, and Lord Alanbrooke now confesses that he intended it to do so.

Once TORCH was accepted as the first rung on a

ladder, planted firmly on the "Imperial Base" in the North African desert, fighting up that ladder would be the best way to pare down German military strength, and pin down German divisions south of the Alps, so that Russia could hold out and an Allied invasion of the Continent in 1944 would be practical. This was a perfectly cogent and defensible strategy; but Sir Alan Brooke disclosed it only bit by bit, which naturally gave the Americans the feeling that they had been "had." Admiral King predicted that, once committed to the Mediterranean, we would be forced to go on and on in that region and never be able to disengage; and he was right.

The American and British landings on North Africa between Safi and Algiers were a tremendous gamble but a brilliant success, largely because the French forces in North Africa quit fighting very quickly, on orders from Admiral Darlan. Operation TORCH, in conjunction with General Montgomery's victory at El Alamein, enabled us to clear the Axis out of all North Africa by May 1943, to reopen the Suez Canal, and secure the Middle East.

But we were unable to resist the military logic of Sir Alan Brooke. After he mounted us on his strategic ladder, the necessity remained to "do something" in 1943, as well as in 1942. So logic compelled us to take the next rungs, invading Sicily (July) and Italy (September) in 1943. This caused the fall of Mussolini and the capitulation of the Italian government. That was supposed to be a great victory for the Allies, but I wonder if it really was. The fall of Italy gave the Germans a chance to take over; they rushed forces into the vacuum left by the surrender, and the Allies embarked on a long, bloody and expensive campaign up the boot of Italy, which ended only with the German surrender in May 1945. I can see the advantage of establishing a military line across Italy to keep German divisions pinned down and off the necks of our forces invading Normandy in 1944; but I cannot see the value of the heavy sacrifices that we made to push the Germans up to the Po. Lord Alanbrooke makes game of the Prime Minister's concept of defeating Germany through Norway, "advancing victoriously over one mountain range after another"; but isn't that precisely what the armies of Wilson, Alexander and Mark Clark were forced to do, although in a somewhat pleasanter climate than that of Norway?

There was a real danger in 1944 that the "secondary" Italian campaign would become the only campaign against Germany that year. Mr. Churchill and the British Chiefs of Staff were constantly pressing the United States to contribute more ships (especially LSTs), aircraft, and troops to the Mediterranean theater, and the Joint Chiefs of Staff had to assume the ungrateful role of watchdogs over Allied resources, lest so much be sent to the Mediterranean that we would find it impossible to lay on the cross-Channel operation in 1944. Lord Alanbrooke's diaries are full of peevish comments about the Americans, especially Admiral King, sending stuff to the Pacific that he wanted to use in Italy. Apparently he would have had us "stop the war" in the Pacific in favor of his favorite campaign up the boot. One can imagine C.I.G.S. exclaiming, as the Empress Eugénie is said to have done in 1870, *"C'est ma guerre, ma petite guerre à moi!"* [6]

[6] Mr. John Ehrman feels that I have not properly described the British strategy in the Mediterranean, and I take pleasure in quoting what he wrote to me on the subject:
"The British strategy for Europe in 1944 was in fact based on arithmetic. Given our weight of assault in the north and the weight of the enemy's defence, a part of that defence *must* be occupied elsewhere. That must be in the south; Italy was the only practical first step in that area; and British ideas for the eastern Mediterranean rested on the possibility of early victory in Italy (by early in '44) and the consequent necessity to maintain pressure somewhere in the south until OVERLORD had been safely launched. Whatever the side comments and temporary

Sir Arthur Bryant, in his reply to my review of *The Turn of the Tide*,[7] states:

"He [Field Marshal Brooke] had shown how, by striking across the Mediterranean, a victory in Europe could be won in 1943 which would fatally strain the enemy's inadequate north-to-south communications, whose capacity, because of the Alpine ranges, was only about a seventh of those from east to west, and compel him to deploy and keep deployed large forces to defend an immense additional stretch of coastline and hold down the restless peoples of southern and southeastern Europe. . . .

"The central strategic problem of the war for the United Nations and Axis alike was that of communications. It was Brooke's consistent grasp of this and of the fact that Britain's and America's lay across the oceans that constitutes his claim to a vision superior to that of his American vis-à-vis. The capture of Sicily and the Italian campaign that followed was only one facet of Brooke's and Britain's Mediterranean strategy; had his American colleagues grasped, instead of so stubbornly opposing, his argument, there would have been no need for a British-American army to fight its way 'over the hard spine of the Appenines,' for the landing craft and

---

deviations, this seems to me to have been the basic strategy. So far from postponing OVERLORD in '44, it was thought to be the only plan which would make OVERLORD possible in '44."

[7] *New York Times Book Review* (30 June 1957).

43

carriers would have been available, as Brooke wished, to land overwhelming forces in the enemy's rear and trap his troops in Italy as they had been trapped in Africa."

My comment on this is: —

(1) The supposed difficulty for the Germans of getting divisions in and out of Italy is an illusion. Reference to Kesselring's memoirs or to any of the detailed works on the Italian campaign show that the Germans were always able to reopen the Brenner Pass after it had supposedly been bombed out of all usefulness, and that they were able to rush reinforcements into Italy, or withdraw them, with little more difficulty than they shifted divisions from the Russian to the French front. Mobility was Kesselring's great forte, and his successor was almost equally good at shifting troops until the very end of the war, when the Allies concentrated a great proportion of their air power on stopping it. The J.C.S., to its credit, saw the hollowness of this argument for the Italian campaign, which is one reason why they opposed it.

(2) It was impossible to make more landing craft and aircraft carriers available for the Italian campaign, because the former were needed in Eng-

land to train for OVERLORD, and the latter were more
urgently needed in the Pacific and on the North
Russian convoy route. If Sir Arthur Bryant's (I
hardly think that they are Lord Alanbrooke's) strategic ideas had prevailed, the Pacific war would have
had to close down, and the cross-Channel operation
would have had to be postponed *sine die*, in order
to make Alanbrooke's *petite guerre* the main campaign of the war. Nor can I see how a series of
Anzio operations could have helped matters, in view
of Kesselring's amazing capacity for swift deployment.

Was it a mistake to have accepted the North
African invasion for 1942, with its logical consequences in Italy? Should the full-scale invasion of
the Continent have been laid on in 1943? Suppose
Operation SLEDGEHAMMER — the small French beachhead in 1942 — had been abandoned, could we
not have concentrated on ROUNDUP in 1943, and
liberated France a year earlier than we did?
It would have been far easier to land in
France in 1943 than in 1944, because in the earlier
year the Germans had not yet built their "Atlantic
wall" of concrete and steel. If the United States had

firmly refused to be drawn into Mediterranean operations, would it have been possible to have defeated Germany in 1944, and ended the war in Europe without that extra year's dependence on Russia which cost us so dear?

On the whole, I think not. In a continental mass like France, the important part of an amphibious operation is not the assault landing, but the build-up and expansion of the beachhead. We could have got ashore with fewer losses in 1943 than were incurred on the beaches in 1944, but the Germans could have concentrated ground and air forces against us quickly and massively, which they were unable to do in 1944, after another year of the air war and of fighting Russia. The American troops for a 1943 invasion would have had to be transported across the North Atlantic when the U-boat menace was at its height. Moreover, if we had not invaded the Mediterranean, the Germans could have assumed the offensive in that area, as Rommel was begging Hitler to do; they might have captured Malta, overrun the Middle East, perhaps dragged Turkey into the war against us, and even knocked Russia out of the war — as had happened, from other causes, in 1917. For Russia had a soft underbelly, on the Black Sea. It is not at all probable that *Landsinnig* Hitler could have been persuaded to launch a Mediterranean diversion when he was at grips with Russia; but a strategic vacuum is always dangerous.

One can debate this strategic question endlessly; but I am satisfied, as Generals Marshall and Eisenhower and the entire J.C.S. were satisfied, that the Anglo-American compromise of concentrating on the Mediterranean in 1942-1943 and pulling off the big cross-Channel operation in 1944 was correct. The Italian campaign did keep German divisions out of France and off the Eastern front, therefore helping OVERLORD to go over and the Russians to advance; but it seems to me that this "pinning down" of German forces could have been accomplished with far less effort if we had not attempted to push the Italian campaign beyond Rome.

7

Operation OVERLORD

It must not be supposed that, once we had yielded the TORCH, as it were, to Churchill, it was easy to get the cross-Channel operation firmed up for 1944. At the Casablanca Conference in January 1943, the Americans succeeded only in getting a vote to set up a Combined Planning Staff. This was done in March, when the able and enthusiastic Lieutenant General Sir Frederick E. Morgan became "Cossac" — Chief of Staff to the Supreme Allied Commander (designate). Not until August 1943, at the Quebec Conference, could the Joint Chiefs of Staff persuade the Combined Chiefs of Staff to accept Cossac's plan for OVERLORD, as the cross-Channel operation had been named; and to declare that it should be the first charge on Allied resources in 1944.

The British Chiefs, especially Sir Alan Brooke, never could seem to understand why the Ameri-

cans had to have commitments well in advance.
They accused us of being rigid and inflexible, not
realizing the terrific job of procurement, shipbuild-
ing, troop training and supply necessary to place a
million and a half troops in England, with armor,
tanks and troop-lift, ready to invade the Continent.

General Wedemeyer had emphasized this at his
first presentation of General Marshall's plan to the
British Chiefs of Staff in April 1942. He kept insisting that we must have a firm date for the invasion of
the Continent in order to work out logistic schedules;
but nobody on the British side, with the important
exception of General Sir Frederick Morgan, seemed
to understand this elementary strategic factor. The
general idea in Britain seems to have been that
America had an inexhaustible pool of manpower,
weapons, landing craft, aircraft and other lethal
weapons which could be deployed at a moment's
notice. American production schedules were upset
in April 1942, to give top priority to landing and
beaching craft for SLEDGEHAMMER, and upset again
in January 1943, to give top priority to destroyer escorts and escort carriers for antisubmarine warfare.
That is why there was an Allied landing and beaching craft shortage in 1944. Admiral King was always

loyal to the major strategic decision, "Beat Germany First," and he thoroughly believed in it, too; but he did not see any sense in piling up men, landing craft and matériel in England while Mr. Churchill and the British Chiefs of Staff were making up their minds what, if anything, would be done with them.

All these elements could in the meantime be better employed in the Pacific to keep the Japanese off balance. Everyone knows that there is nothing worse for troops than to keep them training and drilling for years without combat. The British also learned this, with respect to certain divisions which were kept too long in training camps. The Americans had a similar experience with a National Guard division which was called out in 1940 but not committed in the Pacific for three years, and by that time was of very little use to anyone but the enemy.

As far as planning for our formidable entry into the Continent was concerned, the fourteen months from April 1942 to June 1943 were largely wasted. The main points are that the world-wide shortage of landing and beaching craft, in 1944, of which Chester Wilmot and Sir Arthur Bryant have complained so bitterly, was not caused by an American conspiracy to starve Europe and fatten the Pacific Fleet, but by the shift of production priorities in favor of destroyer escorts and escort carriers, and the long delay in setting a firm date for Operation OVERLORD.

Even after September 1943, when OVERLORD was firmed up for 1944, Mr. Churchill tried to have it postponed, in order to get in some more thrusts around the ring. A landing on the island of Rhodes was one of his schemes in which nobody else could see much sense; but he clung to it even after Roosevelt and Stalin had pointed out at Teheran in December 1943 that it could not be done if we were to cross the Channel in the summer of 1944. At the informal Algiers Conference in January 1944, Mr. Churchill, holding onto the lapels of his coat, after the manner of an orator in the House of Commons, remarked pompously, "His Majesty's government cannot accept the consequences if we fail to make this operation against Rhodes!" To which General Marshall, with an outburst of profanity very unusual for him, replied, "No American is going to land on that goddam island!" And that was that.

Mr. Churchill told an American general in April 1944 that if *he* had been planning OVERLORD, he would have waited until we could have recovered Norway, taken some Aegean islands and got Turkey into the war on our side. General Morgan had some difficulty in inducing his planning staff to take OVER-LORD seriously, because so many of his countrymen hoped it would never be necessary — that something would turn up, such as a crack in German morale, or bombing them into subjection, or the death of Hitler, or what not. I shall await with curiosity what Sir Arthur Bryant will say in his next volume about Field Marshal Brooke's attitude toward OVERLORD, and what the Alanbrooke diaries themselves reveal. C.I.G.S. certainly gave the Americans the impression that he didn't like it, didn't want it, and never believed in it. General Walter Bedell Smith, General Eisenhower's Chief of Staff, has written to me: —

On one occasion, during a conversation I had with him in his office, shortly before I took over the Supreme Headquarters Staff, he expressed himself to the effect that it was not the role of the Western Allies to exert their power on land in Europe — that our power should be utilized in the air and on the sea and that the Russians should do the land fighting. He added that he had fought through the bocage country of Normandy and knew only too well how difficult this terrain was for successful offensive operations.[8]

[8] Quoted by permission. This would have been around 10 January 1944.

Planning for OVERLORD was also hampered by President Roosevelt's delay in appointing a Supreme Commander. From August through December 1943, he was balancing the respective merits of Generals Marshall and Eisenhower, and selected the latter only at Christmastide, when persuaded that Marshall was the key man on the Joint Chiefs of Staff and could not be spared from Washington.

After this appointment of Supreme Commander, which gave the hitherto headless Cossac staff an energetic director, plans and preparations for OVERLORD went along with hardly a hitch. The invasion of the Continent on the ever-famous D-day, 6 June 1944, was a deserved success, so well had it been planned and so perfectly had secrecy as to the date and the target been kept from the enemy.

8

Operation DRAGOON

There was a long and bitter strategic argument over Operation DRAGOON, the concomitant invasion of Southern France. The Allies had insufficient troop-lift to lay it on at the Normandy D-day, so it had to be postponed to 15 August 1944. General Eisenhower insisted on it for two reasons: (1) to get General Patch's Seventh Army and General de Lattre de Tassigny's First French Army deployed on his southern flank for the final invasion of Germany; and (2) to capture the major port of Marseilles for the logistic supply of his armies. Mr. Churchill and the British Chiefs of Staff opposed for two reasons: (1) because troops for DRAGOON would have to be taken from the Italian front, and (2) because they wanted the whole operation diverted to Trieste, in order to send an army up through the Ljubljana Gap, and race the Russians to Budapest and Vienna.

United States Navy planners, and I believe those

of the Royal Navy as well, certainly the American and French generals, were appalled at the idea of shifting this amphibious attack from Marseilles to Trieste, which was a thousand miles farther from Gibraltar than is Marseilles. Eisenhower rejected it, not once and again, but again and again. Both Mr. Churchill and Mr. Hanson Baldwin call the American refusal to consent to this switch of targets one of the major blunders of the war. I emphatically dissent from this view, for two reasons: (1) the troops committed in Southern France, and the great port of Marseilles, were necessary for Eisenhower's final advance into Germany; and (2) the Ljubljana Gap — narrow, tortuous, dominated by mountain peaks — would have been a tactical cul-de-sac. The railway runs through innumerable tunnels which the Germans, who were there in force, could easily have blown; and the road was a two-lane affair, over which the logistical support of more than two divisions would have been impossible. Nor could any such shift of forces as Mr. Churchill wanted have enabled the Western Allies to beat the Russians to Vienna. The Trieste landing, if the Joint Chiefs of Staff had consented to make the shift, could not have been laid on before the end of August, and by the end of August the Russians were already in Bucharest.

Here was a good instance of political considerations impinging on the purely military in a strategic decision. Mr. Churchill appreciated the political value of beating the Russians to the Danube. He regarded this object so paramount that he brushed off as inconsequential the difficulties that geography would force the Western Allies to face. For Mr. Roosevelt, following General Marshall's advice, the strategic advantages of invading Provence rather than Yugoslavia were paramount; and the political arguments that appealed to him were on the same side. As he frankly informed Mr. Churchill, the risk of a popular explosion over the discovery that American divisions were committed to the Balkans instead of supporting Eisenhower, outweighed the dubious chance of winning a race to Budapest or Vienna. Nor could French wishes be ignored. When General de Lattre de Tassigny and General Patch heard the rumor that the invasion of Provence was to be dropped in favor of a Balkan safari, the one wept and the other prayed. The French, all primed to help liberate their own country, were not lightly to be diverted

Emathiam et latos Haemi pinguescere campos.
To fertilize Macedonia and the Balkan plains.

9

Conclusion on Europe

Thus, the Western Allies' strategy for the defeat of Germany was a compromise between General Marshall's plan of concentrating on one major thrust through France not later than 1943, the Churchill concept of pecking away at the perimeter of *Festung Europa* until a weak spot was found, and the Alanbrooke concept of crawling up the Italian boot to the Alps, and then going in for the kill, cross-Channel. The final plan was a sensible compromise. The Mediterranean campaigns did bring substantial benefits, and Operation OVERLORD, in June 1944, had far more skill, power and enthusiasm behind it than ROUNDUP of 1943 could possibly have had. But we shall always think nostalgically of how wonderful it would have been if we could have beaten Germany a year earlier — so many fewer lives lost, so much less destruction; and above all, so much less dependence on Russia.

Once Operation OVERLORD was launched, General Eisenhower had the direction of the strategy, subject always to being overruled by the Combined Chiefs of Staff. More than once he was embarrassed by Field Marshal Montgomery, who had a strategic principle somewhat similar to General MacArthur's — namely, "Let *me* do it." One of these controversies arose over the crossing of the Rhine in 1945. "Monty" proposed to cross first, over the lower Rhine, while the rest of the expeditionary force held the left bank. That did not appeal to "Ike." The strategy of a double envelopment of the Ruhr, in order to destroy Germany's principal center of war production, had been planned by General Marshall since 1942, and Eisenhower now intended to carry it out. The subject came up before the Combined Chiefs of Staff at their Malta meeting in January 1945. Walter Bedell Smith, Eisenhower's Chief of Staff, who attended to present his general's case, ran up against the objections of Field Marshal Sir Alan Brooke, who wished the Combined Chiefs of Staff to adopt the Montgomery plan. Both Smith and Marshall warned the

British Chiefs of Staff that if any such directive were adopted, it would be tantamount to a vote of lack of confidence in Eisenhower, who would feel obliged to resign as Supreme Commander. Marshall handled the matter with his usual tact, and Eisenhower's plans were carried out.

In my opinion the chief American contributions to the strategy of the European war were (1) our faithful adherence to the concept of beating Germany first, "in spite of great temptations" to concentrate on the war against Japan; (2) our insistence on putting over Operation OVERLORD in 1944; and (3) our stand for Operation DRAGOON. But for the insistent, unremitting, often tactless pressure by Roosevelt, Marshall, Eisenhower, and others, to throw great forces across the Channel in June of 1944, there would have been no invasion of Northern Europe that year. It would again have been postponed in favor of more operations in the Mediterranean. And, if we had not invaded Northern Europe in the summer of 1944, London would have been laid flat by the V-1 bombs and V-2 rockets. For no defense at that time had been worked out against the V-2, and without an invasion of Northern Europe its launching sites would have remained intact. Nobody has more respect for the fortitude of the English people than I have; yet could they, after all their previous sufferings and sacrifices, have withstood an accelerated and intensified V-2 offensive?

I I

The War in the Pacific

I

Initial Strategic Blunders

It would be difficult to imagine conditions of warfare more different from those of Europe than those in the Pacific. Instead of thickly populated countries with intensive agriculture, stone dwellings and ancient monuments, countries where ample manpower and limited supplies could be found, you had atolls and islands covered with jungle and scrub, where one could not even count on a supply of fresh water, and where the primitive inhabitants, Micronesians and Melanesians, were, for the most part, indifferent to the war. In the Pacific we had no enthusiastic local allies similar to the *Forces françaises de la Résistance* until we reached the Philippines. Instead of Germans — a tough and cruel but realistic enemy, who recognized certain elementary rules of war, and surrendered readily when surrounded — one had a tough,

63

cruel and fanatical enemy who dug in and had to be exterminated, man by man.

And the distances were vast. It was only 80 miles across the English Channel to the Far Shore, but 4000 miles from Pearl Harbor to Palau, the gateway to the Philippines; and Pearl Harbor itself lies some 2000 miles from the continental United States. In the Western Hemisphere, we thought ourselves lucky when we had a foothold in North Africa, 150 miles from Axis territory. In the Pacific, when we seized Eniwetok, 1000 miles from the Marianas, we felt right on top of the enemy; and if some pessimist remarked, "We've still over 3000 miles to go to Tokyo, old boy," we told him to shut up — the B-29s would make nothing of that.

American strategy in the Pacific, until mid-1942, was wholly defensive; and until 1944, almost entirely naval. As part of the ABC Staff Agreement of 27 March 1941, in the event that we entered the war, the Pacific became an area of American responsibility. Our Joint Army-Navy planners drew up what was called the Rainbow-5 plan, to go into effect if and when we were at war with Japan. The Roosevelt Administration and its military advisers, including General MacArthur, hoped that Japan could be dissuaded by diplomacy from attacking American or British possessions until the spring of 1942. By that time the Fleet would be strengthened by new construction, and the Philippines, provided with a large number of B-17s — the heavy bomber of the day — might be rendered capable of defending themselves. The Rainbow-5 plan called for the United States Pacific Fleet to start across that ocean from Pearl Harbor when war was declared, capture Japanese positions in the Marshall and Caroline Islands, and then proceed to the relief of the Philippines or Singapore or Indonesia, as events required. This fleet movement was estimated to take several months to accomplish. But would the Japanese allow us time to do that?

Of course, as we know, they did not. In great secrecy the Japanese evolved a plan to eliminate the United States Pacific Fleet by a surprise attack on Pearl Harbor, before declaring war; and then by a rapid series of amphibious assaults, to occupy the Philippines, wrest the great naval base of Singapore from the British Empire, conquer Malaya, and Burma, neutralize Thailand and occupy the Dutch colonies. The Japanese war lords thought that they could then establish an impregnable defense barrier running from the Kurile Islands through Wake and the Marshalls, around Indonesia and to the borders of India, maintained by mutually supporting airfields and a highly mobile fleet. Inside this barrier they could organize and exploit the resources of East Asia — the "Greater East Asia Co-Prosperity Sphere" as they called it — and become the strongest military-naval power in the world. It was a strategy of breathtaking boldness, and (let us remember in this age when we are dealing with imponderable forces and improbable contingencies) *it almost worked*. The one thing wrong in Japanese calculation was America's power of recuperation after her Pacific Fleet had been destroyed. They figured that we would simply beat our heads off against their defense barrier and be ready to make peace on the basis of Japan's retaining all conquests up to the international date line. They could then proceed at leisure to complete the conquest of China, after which about half the world's population would be under Japanese control.

America's first contribution in the Pacific theater was a colossal blunder in high strategy. Although the Japanese war lords had made no secret of their goals, these seemed so fantastic that they were not believed; just as many responsible statesmen in Western Europe refused to believe that Hitler meant what he said. The high-ranking officers of the Army and Navy whose duty it was to evaluate Intelligence material, knew, by mid-November, that Japan was about to move south; but whether against the Philippines, Malaya or Indonesia they could not guess. When that southward movement actually began, in the third or fourth week of November, they assumed that it was all; that Japan was incapable of launching another thrust eastward. And those who thought that they knew something about the mind of the Japanese could not believe that they would deliberately bring America into the war, angry and united, at one blow. Thus, Vice Admiral Nagumo's "sneak attack" on Pearl Harbor on a peaceful Sunday, when church bells were ringing in the city and boatswains in the Fleet were piping to morning colors, was a complete surprise, strategic and tactical.

Nevertheless, the Pearl Harbor attack was only a qualified tactical success because no aircraft carrier was sunk, and the installations and fuel tanks at Pearl Harbor were hardly touched. And from a strategic point of view, the thing was idiotic. For, if Japan had attacked only British and Dutch possessions, the American Congress might well have refused to declare war; and if Japan had attacked the Philippines, the Battle Fleet (according to the Rainbow-5 plan) would have gone lumbering across the Pacific, very likely to be sunk in deep water by Japanese bombers based on the Marshall Islands. Japan could have attained all her initial objectives in Southwest Asia before the United States Navy was ready to give battle.

It was long before anyone could appreciate these fundamentals, or foretell the setting of the Rising Sun. For three months after the Pearl Harbor attack the Pacific was practically a Japanese lake. American air bases in the Philippines were bombed a few hours after Pearl Harbor, and our air defenses there were almost completely destroyed. Two key islands in the American system of defenses, Wake and Guam, were taken before the end of the year. The Japanese Army, well supported by the Fleet, made a series of amphibious landings on Luzon, and pushed the greatly outnumbered forces under General MacArthur onto the Bataan Peninsula and the island of Corregidor. Within a few weeks the remnants of General Mac-Arthur's forces, after a brave rear-guard action at Bataan, were forced to surrender. The heaviest units of the British Far Eastern Fleet were sunk by Japa-

nese aërial torpedoes, and Singapore was captured.
The whole of Indonesia — Borneo, Java, Sumatra,
Bali, the Celebes, Halmahera and Dutch New
Guinea — was overrun. Rabaul in the Bismarcks, a
bastion to Australia, was occupied. By 9 March
1942, when the Dutch surrendered Java — three
months and a day after the Pearl Harbor attack — the
Japanese had achieved all their principal aims. They
were the rulers of East Asia, west to British India and
south to the waters adjacent to Australia and Fiji.
India, threatened by nationalists within as by enemies without, and Australia, whither General Mac-
Arthur and a skeleton staff had retired, were trem-
blingly aware that their turn might come next.

The Rainbow-5 plan, rendered unworkable by the
Pearl Harbor attack, was promptly scrapped and
American strategy completely revised. Our situation in the Pacific was roughly parallel to that of
Great Britain after her evacuation of the Continent
at Dunkirk. Just as the most essential thing then for
Britain was to preserve her lifeline to Canada and
the United States, so for us the most essential task
was to protect our Pacific lifelines — the Panama
Canal, through Samoa and the Fijis to New Zealand;
and Pearl Harbor through the Fijis and New Cale-

donia to Australia. America had to be on the strategic defensive until she had accumulated enough forces for an offensive.

Fortunately, for us, the United States Navy still had a carrier striking force — the *Lexington, Enterprise, Yorktown, Hornet,* and *Saratoga* — with which it could strike here and there at the Japanese barrier — at Wake, Gilbert and Marshall Islands, New Britain, etc. This corresponded to the British strategy of lunging around the European periphery. As there, so here, it was a strategy of weakness, not of strength. The most important of these strikes was Jimmy Doolittle's strike on Tokyo by B-25s brought up in carrier *Hornet,* on 18 April 1942. That spectacular raid may be compared, strategically, with the British landing at Dieppe the same summer; it had no importance except as a bucker-up of morale, and probably did us more harm, by putting the enemy on his guard, than it did us good in lessons learned.

2

"Victory Disease"

The old Roman proverb, *quos Deus vult perdere prius dementat*, was never better exemplified than in World War II by General Tojo's strategy of 1942. Flushed with victory, and confident that Germany would conquer Europe, the Japanese war lords succumbed to what some of their own people after the war called the "Victory Disease." Instead of consolidating their immense conquests of the first few months of war, and concentrating on a defensive strategy, they embarked on a new program of conquest, as follows: —

1. To capture Tulagi in the Solomons and Port Moresby, the capital of Papua, New Guinea, in order to dominate the Coral Sea and threaten Australia.

2. To capture Midway Island and the Western Aleutians, in order to enlarge the defensive perimeter, bring the United States Pacific Fleet to a decisive engagement, and destroy what was left of it after Pearl Harbor.

3. To capture New Caledonia, the Fijis and Samoa, in order to cut the lifelines between the United States and the Antipodes.

In the first phase, Tulagi was taken but the capture of Port Moresby was frustrated by the Battle of the Coral Sea. In the second phase, the Japanese had their wish of provoking a major fleet action, the great Battle of Midway; but it turned out very differently from what they had hoped and expected. Hence the third phase, the conquest of New Caledonia, Fijis and Samoa, was never attempted.

Admiral Yamamoto, greatest of the Japanese sea lords since Togo, and the one who had planned the strike on Pearl Harbor, was responsible for the strategy of seeking a major fleet action immediately. He figured out that the United States Pacific Fleet was being so rapidly reinforced by new construction, that it must be completely smashed in 1942; next year would be too late. Having smashed it, Japan could then set up air patrols between the Aleutians, Wake, Midway, the Gilberts and Marshalls and the Solomons; and with Midway Island in her possession, the great American naval base at Pearl Harbor, whose installations had unaccountably been neglected in the attack of 7 December 1941, could be bombed into impotence. The Japanese Navy would be able to cruise at will over the vast reaches of the Pacific, and land troops anywhere that might seem expedient — in Australia, for instance.

The Battle of the Coral Sea on 8 May 1942, first of three carrier air battles in which no ship of either side sighted one of the other, turned back the Japanese transports which were to have taken Port Moresby, Papua. From the Japanese point of view, however, Coral Sea was but a right hook before the "sockdolager" with their left, at Midway, less than a month later. Admiral Yamamoto brought almost the entire Japanese Navy across the Pacific with the triple purpose of occupying the Western Aleutians, occupying Midway Island, and engaging the United States Pacific Fleet. That Fleet was then a David to Yamamoto's Goliath; but Admirals Spruance and Fletcher, with perfect tactics, knocked the heart out of the Japanese by sinking four large carriers, and Yamamoto retired, frustrated. Never again did the Japanese regain the offensive. But the concept of "one decisive naval battle" remained in their minds until they had no navy left.

Japan still held Tulagi in the Solomons and Rabaul in the Bismarcks. These were the anchors to a really formidable barrier — the Bismarcks Barrier — because the islands are so close to one another that the surrounding waters could be controlled by land-based planes. Admiral King in Washington, Admiral Nimitz at Pearl Harbor, and General MacArthur at Brisbane decided that this barrier must be broken or breached if ever we were to defeat Japan. The start of this campaign was expedited by the news that the Japanese were building an airfield on Guadalcanal, whence they would be able to batter our advance base at Nouméa, New Caledonia. On 7 August 1942, United States Marines landed at Tulagi and Guadalcanal, surprised the enemy, and seized the harbor of the one and the airfield of the other.

There then began the prolonged and bloody struggle for Guadalcanal; an island worthless in itself but violently contested. The Japanese could not afford to let us establish a base there and we could not afford to let it go. Ships, planes and troops were committed by both sides. Six violent naval battles were fought, until Iron Bottom Bay, as our sailors named Savo Island Sound, was strewn with the hulls of ships and the bodies of sailors. On shore, the Marines fought stubbornly and, in the end, successfully. By 9 February 1943, six months after the landings, the Japanese were forced to evacuate Guadalcanal.

3

The Strategic Bargain at Casablanca

At the time of the Casablanca Conference of the
Combined Chiefs of Staff with President Roosevelt and
the Prime Minister, in January 1943, the Pacific strategy of the United States, aimed primarily at breaking
the Bismarcks Barrier, had progressed only to the extent of gaining air and sea control of the Southern Solomons. Admiral King and General Marshall, at Casablanca, pointed out that only fifteen per cent of total
Allied resources in ships, troops and weapons were
then being deployed in the Pacific. They argued
that, although we were and intended to remain faithful to the concept of beating Germany first, it would
be fatal to lose the initiative we had won against
Japan, and to try to make it a holding war, as Lord
Alanbrooke apparently wished us to do. From the
Alanbrooke Diaries it is clear to me[1] (though not to

---

[1] *The Turn of the Tide* (American edition, 1957) pp. 401, 440,
492-493, 501, 507-508, 533-535, 572, 587.

their editor) that C.I.G.S. resented any American forces being sent to the Pacific. It would seem that he expected the Japanese to stay put until the war in Europe was over, when the Anglo-American Allies could deploy their entire strength in the Pacific. This strategy has a delightful eighteenth-century flavor; but I cannot imagine that the "Gentlemen of Japan" would have coöperated by saying politely, *"Messieurs les Alliés, tirez les premiers!"*

The Casablanca Conference resulted in a strategic bargain. The J.C.S. agreed to step up another rung of the Mediterranean ladder, and, tacitly, to postpone the cross-Channel operation to 1944. The B.C.S. abandoned their opposition to America's assuming the offensive in the Pacific. They agreed that the J.C.S. should settle the details of operations against Japan, subject to the approval of the Combined Chiefs of Staff for plans that required a new allocation of fighting power. The formula agreed upon, drafted by Air Marshal Sir John Slessor, stated, "Operations in the Pacific and Far East shall continue with the forces allocated, with the object of maintaining pressure on Japan, retaining the initiative and attaining a position of readiness for the full-scale offensive against Japan by the United Nations as soon as Germany is defeated. These operations must be kept within such limits as will not, in the opinion of the Combined Chiefs of Staff, prejudice the capacity of the United Nations to take any opportunity that may present itself for the decisive defeat of Germany in 1943." [2]

[2] Sir John Slessor *The Central Blue* (Cassell and Co. Ltd., London, 1956) p. 446.

4

American Deployment in the Pacific and in Europe Compared

Thereafter, American planners had things much their own way in the Pacific. Fortunately, the Pacific war could be fought to a great extent with different ships and weapons from those that were wanted in the European war, and with fewer ground troops and aircraft. By the end of 1943, the United States had deployed ground and air forces as follows:[3]

In Europe:	1,416,485 men	17 divisions	8,237 aircraft
In the Pacific:	912,942 "	13 "	4,254 "

And please remember that in the Pacific we carried almost the entire burden, while in Europe we had two powerful Allies.

The United States shipped overseas somewhat over 1,800,000 men during the first nine months of 1944.

[3] Matloff *Strategic Planning for Coalition Warfare* (U.S. Army Series) Vol. II chap. xiv.

Over seventy-five per cent of these were sent to Europe. By 1 October 1944 the United States had 40 divisions in Europe and the Mediterranean, with 4 more en route: no troops had been sent to the Pacific since 1 August. On that date (1 October 1944) the United States had 57 air groups, and 27 divisions (21 Army, 6 Marine Corps), with 1,314,931 men all told, deployed in the Pacific to defeat Japan, as against 149 air groups and 40 Army divisons, with over 2,750,000 men all told, deployed in Europe and the Mediterranean.

Both the Atlantic and the Pacific theaters of the war were hungry for beaching and landing craft and long-range bombers, and the only serious disputes between the Americans and the British over allocation came over these types. Since Sir Arthur Bryant, like the cry of the whippoorwill, is ever repeating a shortage of "landing craft, landing craft, landing craft" as excuse for the slow progress of the Italian campaign, the reader is requested to glance at this table of the numbers of American and British beaching and landing craft that were *serviceable* and *operational* in different theaters of the war on 1 June 1944:[4]

[4] Morison *The Invasion of France and Germany* (History of U.S. Naval Operations World War II Vol. XI) p. 57. The first three columns of the larger types are what we call beaching craft;

	LST	LCI(L)	LCT	LCM	LCVP	LCA
U.S. in 12th Fleet (U. Kingdom)	168	124	247	216	1089	0
British in United Kingdom	61	121	664	265	0	646
U.S. in Mediterranean	23	59	44	185	395	0
British in Mediterranean	2	32	64	95	0	138
U.S. on East Coast, U.S.A.	95	89	58	57	341	0
U.S. on West Coast, U.S.A.	0	41	1	60	181	0
U.S. in All Pacific Areas	102	128	140	1198	2298	0
British on E. Indies Station	0	4	2	67	0	46

There was a world-wide shortage of these vessels and craft in 1944. That was due to the shifting of top priority in production schedules from landing craft to escort carriers and destroyer escorts, in consequence of the decision at Casablanca that anti-submarine warfare was to be first charge on Allied resources.

Thus, the war in the Pacific was not a drag on the war in Europe, and the complaints of certain British writers about niggardly allocations of American forces and matériel to the European theater show a misunderstanding of the amounts of each that were available. But it is also true that the long delay in establishing a firm date for Operation OVERLORD allowed the American offensive against Japan to de-

---

but British writers generally lump them with the smaller types, which could be carried on davits, as landing craft. Only the most significant types are shown in the above table, which is taken from Combined Staff Planners memo. for Information no. 24, dated 19 June 1944.

velop at a quicker pace. The Pacific theater was supposed to be secondary; but planners could not keep a secondary theater secondary as long as there was no definite or accepted long-range plan for the primary theater. Yet, as early as March 1943, at a conference with American Army and Navy commanders, General Marshall placed a curb on enthusiasts who wanted more troops in the China-Burma-India area in the Southwest Pacific. Throughout the rest of that year, even before OVERLORD was firmed up, he succeeded in reserving the bulk of Army divisions for the invasion of Germany.

The object of those who wanted more troops sent to the China-Burma-India theater was to afford more help to Chiang Kai-shek. Throughout the war, China counted heavily in American strategic calculations. President Roosevelt and General Marshall believed that if Chiang were properly supported, China might become an ally in the Pacific comparable in fighting strength to Russia in Europe. Mr. Churchill, on the contrary, regarded Chiang as a slender reed, and help to China as a waste of men and resources. Mr. Roosevelt's playful suggestion that Britain present Hong Kong to China as a compliment was not well received at 10 Downing Street;

and everyone, including the Communists, must now be glad that it was not taken seriously! As we now know, Mr. Churchill's estimate of Chiang was right and Mr. Roosevelt's was wrong. The Generalissimo of Nationalist China is a very estimable gentleman, always a faithful friend to the Western Allies; but for reasons too complicated to be discussed here, he was of very little value in the war against Japan. It may, however, be pointed out that the only alternative to helping Chiang was to put our money on the Reds, which would merely have brought the Chinese Communists, with their fanatical enmity to Western civilization, into power somewhat earlier than they actually attained it.

5

Four Roads to Tokyo

The strategic problem in the Pacific was vitally different from that in Europe by virtue of distance. Instead of a *Festung Europa* which began within a hundred miles of England, and the breaching of which offered a direct road to victory, you had to deal with a *Festung Nippona* which lay 3400 miles from Pearl Harbor and 3600 miles from Brisbane. This *Festung* was protected by a powerful Navy, by two or three concentric island barriers well supplied with airfields; and it drew on the abundant resources of China, Malaya and Indonesia.

Thus, the main strategic question was how to get at Japan; for nobody then anticipated that Japan could be defeated without an invasion of her home islands. There were four possible routes: —

(1) A comeback through the Indian Ocean and the Straits of Malacca, led by the British Fleet. This

would be impossible unless Admiral Lord Mount-batten, British Commander in the Far East, were given enough force to eject the Japanese from Burma; and that he never did get. (I wish here to say that in my opinion, and that of many Americans who knew him, Mountbatten was one of the ablest strategists of the war in both major theaters, but he was never in a position to prove himself.)

(2) The short route by the Aleutians. This was ruled out as a major line of advance by the constant foul weather in those latitudes, although we did find it necessary to wrest Attu from the Japanese and to force them to evacuate Kiska.

(3) A creep-up on Japan by what General Mac-Arthur called the "New Guinea-Mindanao Axis." This plan, which General MacArthur consistently urged the Joint Chiefs of Staff to adopt, would mean concentrating the entire weight of the Pacific Fleet and amphibious forces under his command, and liberating the Philippines before advancing on Japan.

(4) The Navy's plan for an advance through the Central Pacific, taking the key points in the Gilbert, Marshall, and Caroline Islands en route, then to the Marianas, then Formosa, and creating a base on the coast of China for the final onslaught on Japan.

The argument over ways and means to defeat Japan took place largely within the Joint Chiefs of Staff. Neither General MacArthur nor Admiral Nimitz, whose views were opposed until mid-1944, were members of the J.C.S.; but Nimitz and Admiral King saw generally eye-to-eye, while General Marshall and General MacArthur did not. MacArthur on occasion sent General Sutherland, his Chief of Staff, to present his views to the J.C.S., and General Marshall did his best to be fair to MacArthur, who had been senior to him in the old Army. But there is no denying the fact that the Navy was much better represented in the Joint Chiefs of Staff as respects the conduct of the war in the Pacific than was the Army or the Air Force. The Pacific war was, by and large, the Navy's war, to which the Army conformed. An exception may be made of the Southwest Pacific theater, where Commander Seventh Fleet was seldom admitted to General MacArthur's strategic staff discussions; he was simply told that the General intended to land at such a place on such a date, and the Navy must lift so many troops and see that their movement to the objective was properly covered.

The plan finally adopted for the defeat of Japan was a combination of Numbers 3 and 4, of the Mac-

Arthur and the Navy plans. If you will look at the map you can see that the Marianas, the Carolines, the Marshalls and Gilberts make a series of great spider webs — "made to order for Japan," as one Japanese admiral said, to catch any unwary flies that tried to cross the Pacific. These islands and atolls had been well provided with airfields, advanced naval bases and strong garrisons. The distances between them were so narrow that Japan could fleet up aircraft and naval forces at will. General MacArthur believed that it would take too long to slice through this series of spider webs; we must get around them. Hence his "New Guinea-Mindanao Axis" plan, which required only one big corridor, through the Solomons and Bismarcks.

Admirals King and Nimitz, on the other hand, argued against the MacArthur plan as the sole route of advance, both because it was too roundabout and because it would be subject to devastating flank attacks by aircraft and warships as long as the spider webs remained in Japanese hands. To concentrate on the southwestern route would leave the enemy free to maneuver over the greater part of the Pacific. Moreover, if the Allies adopted a single line of advance, the enemy would naturally concentrate against it; whilst parallel offensives would deceive him as to our ultimate intentions. Thus, the Navy favored a simultaneous advance over both routes, the Central Pacific and the New Guinea-Mindanao Axis, mopping up the spider webs as we proceeded.

6

The Master Plan for the Defeat of Japan

A temporary agreement was reached in the Strategic Plan for the Defeat of Japan adopted by the Combined Chiefs of Staff, on recommendation of the Joint Chiefs of Staff, at Washington in May 1943. This was a compromise between the MacArthur and the Navy plans, pointing towards China as an eventual base for the invasion of the Japanese home islands. As soon as the Bismarcks Barrier was broken, a bridgehead secured in Burma, and strategic islands in the Gilberts and Marshalls secured to protect our flanks, massive forces under MacArthur's command would roll over the back of the New Guinea bird into the Celebes and South China seas, while the British recaptured Singapore. Together we could then recover the Philippines and Hong Kong and establish bases in China for the invasion of Japan.

This master plan was never carried out beyond

the initial phases for several good reasons. (1) The British were unable to undertake the invasion of Burma, since Admiral Mountbatten's amphibious forces in the Indian Ocean were cannibalized to feed the ever-hungry maw of the Mediterranean. (2) The Japanese in May 1943 started an offensive in China, along the Hankow-Hanoi Railway, incidentally seizing the airfields being used by General Chennault's bombers and pushing back into the interior Chiang's forces, on which we had counted to act as interference on the China coast. Thus, the prospects of establishing bases on the China coast became remote.

There was a pause in the Pacific for five months in the first half of 1943 before the United States resumed the offensive. The principal reason for this delay was our lack of aircraft carriers. We had lost *Lexington* at the Coral Sea, *Yorktown* at Midway, *Hornet* and *Wasp* in the Solomons; only *Enterprise* and *Saratoga* were left. When the *Essex*-class carriers, answer to the Pacific sailors' prayer, started to come out, we were ready to go.

During this pause there were fleet and troop movements as far north as the Bering Sea. Among Lord Alanbrooke's many complaints to his diary (and now to the public) of America's wasting manpower and matériel in the Pacific, those about the Aleutians have some justification. No operations in this region of almost perpetual mist and snow accomplished anything of great importance or had any appreciable effect on the outcome of the war. It was a theater of military frustration. Both sides would have done well to have left the Aleutians to the few Aleuts unfortunate enough to live in them. They were United States territory, and the only reason we paid any attention to them was that the Japanese, in their expansive mood of early 1942, directed a carrier raid on Dutch Harbor, the American naval base in Unalaska in the Eastern Aleutians, and occupied Attu and Kiska, the two westernmost islands. These were intended as northern anchors to the Japanese defensive perimeter; and as such, American strategists felt obliged to set them adrift. Attu, the westernmost island, was recaptured by an American amphibious force in April and May 1943, at a cost of some 1800 casualties; and Kiska, about 150 miles east of Attu, was occupied by a Canadian-American amphibious force in August, after the Japanese garrison had evacuated it under cover of fog. This bloodless (and somewhat ridiculous) operation at least illustrated the strategic principal that no island garrison can long hold out if cut off by sea and by air; it strengthened the movement for the "leapfrogging" advance, which we shall mention shortly.

American naval and military commanders in this area now proposed to use the Western Aleutians as a springboard to capture Paramushiro, the Japanese base in the Kuriles; but the Joint Chiefs of Staff denied it. For the possession of this Kurile Island base would confer no benefit on the Allies unless it were exploited for a further advance into Hokkaido, northernmost of the Japanese home islands; and that had been already rejected by the Combined Chiefs of Staff as too expensive. Airdromes were developed on Adak and Attu, in the hope that Russia would shortly declare war on Japan, when these islands might be useful in the chain of communications. During the rest of the war very little happened in this area, except occasional air raids on and one naval bombardment of Paramushiro, and a few, feeble Japanese retaliating raids on the American bases.

7

Offensive Operations Begin

The first phase of the offensive opened in June 1943, with parallel movements from Australia and the South Pacific to break the Bismarcks Barrier. General MacArthur's forces (American and Australian), supported by the Seventh Fleet, whipped around the tail of the New Guinea bird and secured Papua. Admiral Halsey's South Pacific forces (which were under Nimitz) wrested Munda airfield in the Central Solomons from the Japanese and established a beachhead and airfield on Empress Augusta Bay, Bougainville, whence Rabaul, center of the Bismarcks spider web, could be bombed. In both sets of operations, MacArthur's and Halsey's, a new strategy of "leapfrogging" was adopted; and it is still a matter of debate whether this was thought up by General MacArthur or by Admiral Wilkinson, Halsey's amphibious force commander. Wilkinson described this method as "hitting 'em where they ain't" — a baseball term (possibly also comprehensible to cricket enthusiasts) which meant batting the ball into a part of the grounds where no outfielder could possibly retrieve it. In terms of oceanic warfare it meant that instead of invading every island where there was a Japanese garrison, we bypassed the strongest concentrations, such as Rabaul and Wewak, landed amphibious forces where there were comparatively few Japanese, built an airfield, and, using our sea supremacy to cut off the bypassed enemy garrisons, left them to "wither on the vine." General Tojo, after the war was over, told General MacArthur that leapfrogging was one of the three principal factors that defeated Japan, the other two being the attrition of Japanese shipping by American submarines, and the ability of our *Essex*-class carriers to operate for weeks and months without entering harbor for replenishment.

The Japanese counterstrategy, which they called the "New Operational Policy" of September 1943, was to fortify a new defensive perimeter from Saipan through Truk and the Bismarcks to Timor, to delay and wear down the American and Australian offensives, maintain the East Indian frontier with strong ground forces (for Tojo, like Hitler, was land-minded and thought the next major offensive would come from India), and get ready to catch the United States Pacific Fleet unawares when covering an amphibious operation.

We never gave the Japanese a chance to take a stand on this new defensive barrier, but kept them continually off balance, with one lethal blow after another. By the end of February 1944, after successive leapfrogs in the Central and Southwest Pacific, we had secured the Gilbert and Marshall Islands, and broken the Bismarcks Barrier. Bypassing Rabaul was a master stroke; for, as we found at the end of the war, the Japanese commander there had almost 100,000 troops well dug in and provisioned, itching for a chance to give us a hot reception if we had attempted to land. Rabaul was the one place in the Pacific where an amphibious operation might well have been repulsed.

Once the Bismarcks Barrier was broken we gave the enemy no rest. MacArthur's forces pushed on to the conquest of the Admiralties, where Seeadler Harbor, Manus, became a great forward fleet base; to Hollandia, where an important airdrome was built; and along the entire northwest coast of New

Guinea. At the same time, Admiral Nimitz's forces drove into the Marianas — Saipan, Tinian, and Guam.

But we are anticipating events. Before these operations occurred in the spring and early summer of 1944, General MacArthur made a last attempt to have the entire Pacific Fleet committed to his New Guinea-Mindanao Axis. He was denied this privilege for several good reasons: (1) No help was forthcoming from the Royal Navy in that area, owing to the scrapping of the Burma operation. (2) Admiral Nimitz's fast carrier forces, far-running and hard-hitting, were not suitable for employment in the narrow waters south of the Philippines, with Japanese air bases on either side. (3) The B-29 long-range bombers, about to come into operation, could bomb Japan itself if based at Saipan, and (4) Saipan would make an ideal advanced base for our submarines, which with new and more effective torpedoes had really got into their stride and were reducing Japanese merchant tonnage almost daily.

8

Revised Plan for Defeating Japan, December 1943

So the Joint Chiefs of Staff reverted to a combination of the MacArthur and the Navy plans. The rest of the American Pacific strategy is based on a concept presented by the J.C.S. and approved by the C.C.S. at Cairo on 3 December 1943. The objective there was stated to obtain bases "from which the unconditional surrender of Japan can be forced." "The advance along the New Guinea-N.E.I.-Philippines Axis will proceed concurrently with operations for the capture of the Mandated Islands" (the Marianas and Carolines). "A strategic bombing force will be established in Guam, Tinian and Saipan for strategic bombing of Japan proper." The J.C.S. directive of 12 March 1944 to Nimitz and MacArthur was more specific. General MacArthur would continue his advance along western New Guinea; Truk to be neutralized by fast carrier strikes; occupation of the Marianas by Central Pacific forces starting 15 June, and of Mindanao by MacArthur, supported by the Pacific Fleet, on 15 November 1944. It was left open whether we would try to liberate the whole or a part of the Philippines, or go straight from Mindanao and the Marianas into Formosa.

Saipan, Tinian and Guam were captured in a series of brilliant amphibious operations in June and July, while Normandy was being invaded in Europe; and for the second time of the war, and the first time since the Battle of Midway (June 1942), almost the entire Japanese Fleet came out to engage the Pacific Fleet, then under the tactical command of Admiral Spruance. For three days the great carrier battle of the Philippine Sea was fought. It resulted in a brilliant victory for us, despite the escape of most of the Japanese ships, because their air groups were utterly destroyed in the famous "Marianas Turkey Shoot." And from this loss the Japanese Navy never recovered.

9

Philippines or Formosa?

The disagreement between General MacArthur
and Admiral King, as to whether the liberation of the
Philippines should precede or follow the defeat of
Japan, was not wholly resolved until nearly the end
of 1944. The Navy wished to go directly into Formosa
from Saipan and Mindanao, bypassing all the other
Philippine islands; and then seek a base in the
Ryukyus, for the final assault on Japan. Concurrently it planned to strike Japan repeatedly by sending B-29s "up the ladder of the Bonins." General
MacArthur was still intent on liberating the Philippines, and using Luzon for the final or semifinal
springboard to Japan. He made the strong emotional
argument that the United States was honor bound
to liberate the Philippines, where he had been nour-
ishing resistance forces against the Japanese puppet
government, at the earliest possible date; and that if

we failed the Filipinos, no Asiatic would ever trust us. He also made the sound strategic argument that loyal Luzon, sealed off by our sea power, would be a more suitable base to gather forces for the final assault on Japan than hostile Formosa, which the Japanese could easily reinforce from the mainland. To General MacArthur, it appeared as monstrous to defeat Japan before liberating the Philippines, as it would have to General De Gaulle to defeat Germany before liberating France.

Here is an instance where political considerations influenced strategy, and rightly so. General MacArthur's arguments were irrefutable. Happily, his strategic plan, too, was sound, even if stripped of its political overtones. From what we learned of the defenses of Formosa after the war, it would have been a very difficult island upon which to obtain a lodgement, much less a complete conquest. And its contemplated use as a steppingstone to the mainland would not have materialized, since by that time Japan firmly controlled the entire coast of China.

The first approach to a decision on this knotty question was made at Pearl Harbor in the last week of July 1944, at a conference between President Roosevelt, General MacArthur and Admiral Nimitz.

Admiral King, then on a tour of inspection in the Pacific, was very pointedly not invited, for the President already knew his ideas and wished to give Mac-Arthur a free field to expose his views. In this conference the General not only converted the willing President, but the dubious Admiral Nimitz, to his concept — "Leyte, then Luzon." An understanding was reached, not a decision; but, as in the case of the Mediterranean, when once you put your foot on a strategic ladder it is difficult to get off, unless the enemy throws you off. Admiral King and Rear Admiral Forrest Sherman (Admiral Nimitz's top planner), might still argue in the J.C.S. for bypassing Luzon, and throw ridicule on General MacArthur's contention that Manila could be captured in two weeks after a landing at Lingayen; they lost their case.

At the Quebec Conference in September 1944, the following timetable was drawn up by the Combined Chiefs of Staff. I am simplifying it by letting "Mac-Arthur" stand for all Southwest Pacific forces, American and Australian; and "Nimitz" stand for all Central Pacific forces; and I am including operations already authorized, some of which had already started.

15 September: MacArthur to take Morotai, Nimitz to take Peleliu.

5 October: Nimitz to take Yap in the Carolines, and Ulithi a few days later.

15 October: MacArthur to move into Talaud.

15 November: MacArthur to occupy Sarangani Bay, Mindanao.

20 December: MacArthur and Nimitz in concert to invade Leyte.

But it was still left open whether the securing of Leyte would be followed by a landing on Luzon, or on Formosa.

Within a week this timetable was torn up, the plan changed, and the tempo of advance accelerated, owing to Admiral Halsey's carrier raids on the Philippines in September 1944. His *Essex*-class carriers steamed up to within sight of shore, pounded Japanese airfields and destroyed the few Japanese planes that they encountered. These carrier strikes disposed of the myth created by the land-based airmen (counterparts of the British "bomber barons") to the effect that aircraft carriers could not safely venture within flight distance of enemy airfields. In consequence of the revealed air weakness of the enemy in the Philippines, Admiral Halsey, after consulting MacArthur, sent a message via Nimitz to the Joint Chiefs of Staff, then sitting at Quebec with the British Chiefs of Staff, the President, the Prime Minister, and Mr. Mackenzie King. Halsey recommended that the Peleliu, Morotai, Yap and Mindanao operations be cancelled, and that Nimitz and MacArthur make a joint assault on Leyte on 20 October, two months ahead of schedule. General Marshall received MacArthur's consent on the night of 15 September when he and the Joint Chiefs of Staff were being entertained by Canadian officers at the Château Frontenac, Quebec. The Joint Chiefs of Staff interrupted their dinner to confer; and in an hour and a half the decision was made.

General MacArthur and Admiral Nimitz were directed to execute the Leyte operation on 20 October, and Admiral Wilkinson's amphibious force, already embarking to take the Caroline Islands of Peleliu and Yap, was ordered to join them after taking Peleliu.

This sudden change of objectives and of timing was a notable instance of strategic flexibility. The British might have remarked, and doubtless did, Why do you Americans act flexible as a rubber band in the Pacific, and stiff as an iron bar in the Atlantic?

The answer is given by the different circumstances. By mid-1944 the Pacific Fleet and amphibious forces and the MacArthur Army and Seventh Fleet, poised in their advanced bases, were complete, trained and ready to be thrown in anywhere, with the fast, formidable carrier forces (under Rear Admiral Mitscher) ready to run interference. In Europe, for a major assault on the Continent, one needed at least a year's notice to get the men and matériel out to England and trained there. In the Pacific, the men and matériel were already there — at Pearl Harbor, Kwajalein, Eniewetok, Saipan, the Admiralties and Hollandia; and most of the men had been "blooded" in earlier assaults. It made very little difference whether Admiral Wilkinson's amphibious force landed over the coral reefs at Yap, or on the coral beaches at Dulag, Leyte. The logistic plan, of course, required agonizing changes, but that was done; and the amphibious assault on Leyte was one of the most successful of the war.

Another important decision at Quebec in September, 1944, had to do with the entry of the Royal Navy into the Pacific after the defeat of Germany, which most strategists at that particular moment thought would take place before the end of the year. The

British Chiefs of Staff for a year or more had been discussing plans for this participation. These projects are minutely described in a book that I heartily recommend, Volume V of John Ehrman's *Grand Strategy;* so I need say no more of them here than to quote Mr. Ehrman's sententious remark that they were completely unrealistic because based on "the constant and wishful assumption" that American offensive operations in the Pacific would be held up awaiting the arrival of the British. The United States view of the Royal Navy's role was for it to operate eastward from the Indian Ocean, come roaring through Sunda Strait, recapture Singapore and help roll up the Japanese Empire from the south. This concept was pleasing neither to Mr. Churchill nor to the First Sea Lord, Admiral Sir Dudley Pound, nor to his relief, Admiral Lord Cunningham. They wished the Royal Navy to get into the thick of the fighting alongside the United States Navy as it approached the Japanese home islands, and Mr. Churchill was more interested in liberating Hong Kong than in recapturing Singapore of unpleasant memories. General MacArthur did not want the Royal Navy under his command unless it were in the form of a task force attached to the United States

Seventh Fleet, under Admiral Kinkaid, in whom he had great confidence. Admiral King did not want the Royal Navy in the Central Pacific at any price; and said so, in his most unpleasant manner, creating unnecessary offense. Since this was the first time in history that anyone declared he wanted no part of the Royal Navy, the name of Ernest J. King has become anathema in England — somewhat like that of Paul Jones in the eighteenth century; and his attitude does require some explanation.

It was not that King was anti-British, or that he disliked sharing the anticipated spoils of a Pacific victory. The root of his objections was, purely and simply, logistics. Ships of the Royal Navy were what Americans called "short-legged" — that is, they were accustomed to putting into a base for replenishment and upkeep about every two weeks. American ships were "long-legged" — they were staffed with technicians capable of making extensive repairs at sea, and could fuel at sea while making twelve to fifteen knots' speed. For the Fast Carrier Forces Pacific Fleet there had been developed a Mobile Service Base of auxiliary craft which provided the fighting ships with everything they needed at sea, from replacement aircraft and spare engines to cigarettes, so that these vessels could, and did, keep the sea literally for months. As one of our logistics officers said, the services of this floating base were limited only by the available supply of manila line to pass the stuff from an auxiliary vessel to a combatant! Since the Royal Navy did not enjoy these facilities, Admiral King feared it would become a drain on us for logistic supply.

President Roosevelt, for the sake of preserving good Anglo-American relations, overruled the Admiral's objections and required American planners to find a place for a British Fleet in the final operations against Japan in 1945. That they did; and our Pacific Fleet was grateful for Royal Navy support at Okinawa and later.

10

The Battle for Leyte Gulf

The Japanese reacted to our invasion of Leyte by making their third attempt to catch the Pacific Fleet unawares; and for the third time, it was ready for them. Imperial Headquarters committed almost the entire Japanese Navy against Halsey and Kinkaid, with an ingenious but futile plan. Between 23 and 25 October, 1944, they fought the Battle for Leyte Gulf, the greatest naval battle of all time, measured by the forces engaged, and one of the most decisive. The Japanese really had no chance of success, as they had no carrier-based planes and few land-based planes left, and very bad communications between their disparate forces. But they made a good try. Admiral Ozawa's fast carrier fleet inveigled Admiral Halsey's fast carrier groups up north out of the way, and sacrificed itself in the Battle of Cape Engaño, while the main Japanese Fleet under Admiral Kurita, including the two super-battleships

Musashi and *Yamato* with 18.1-inch guns, made a stab at the amphibious forces unloading off Leyte. Kurita was delayed, and induced to turn back, by two escort carrier groups under Rear Admiral T. L. Sprague, in the Battle off Samar — one of the most gallant actions of the war. In the small hours of the same morning a third Japanese fleet had been destroyed in a night action in Surigao Strait by Admiral Oldendorf's old battleships which had been rebuilt and modernized since their sinking in December 1941 — an appropriate revenge for Pearl Harbor.

Although discussion of an actual battle is a tactical matter which I cannot enter into here, there were some interesting strategic issues involved in the Battle for Leyte Gulf. Just as Clausewitz taken out of context or misunderstood has created the mischievous strategic shibboleth that destruction of the enemy's army is the true objective of land warfare, so Mahan taken out of context or misunderstood has supported another bad principle, that the main object of a navy at all times should be to destroy the enemy's fleet.[5] In the Battle of the Philippine Sea,

[5] Captain Bern Anderson and I recently combed through the works of Mahan to try to find a statement to this effect. The nearest we could come to one is in his *Naval Strategy* p. 199,

in June 1944, Admiral Spruance was vigorously criticized because at a crucial point he reversed course to cover the amphibious operation at Saipan, which was his primary mission, and lost an opportunity to destroy Admiral Ozawa's carrier fleet. Consequently, Admiral Halsey's orders from Admiral Nimitz prior to the Leyte operation contained a clause to the effect that he was to lose no opportunity to smash the enemy's fleet. Halsey, of a naturally aggressive temperament, took this very much to heart and regarded it as his main and overriding mission. That would have been all right if his Intelligence had rightly informed him as to what was the principal Japanese fleet. But it did not; hence he took his carriers, with their powerful screen of new battleships, heavy cruisers and destroyers, up north in pursuit of Ozawa's carriers — almost bare of planes and out merely as a decoy — leaving the entrance to San Bernardino Strait unguarded. The consequences might have been very serious but for the tough fight put up by the Sprague escort carriers, and the indecision and timidity of Admiral Kurita.

where in discussing the Siege of Gibraltar he says, "In war the proper main objective of the navy is the enemy's navy." But see pp. 220-221 of the same work, where he indicates that this is not to be considered an absolute.

On the Japanese side they violated another strategic shibboleth, "never divide your forces," but they did that of necessity. The main part of their Fleet had been sent to Lingga Roads off Singapore to be near its fuel supply (American submarines having sunk most of the Japanese tankers), while the carriers stayed in the Inland Sea to train new air groups.

The lesson is that in warfare no strategic principles are absolutes; that in any operation the nature of his mission should be the commanding officer's guide. And the outstanding tactical lesson of the Battle for Leyte Gulf is the utter helplessness of a modern fleet without air support. That is why "jeep carriers" screened by destroyer escorts were able, off Samar, to defeat a surface fleet of battleships, heavy cruisers, and destroyers. Halsey's earlier strikes on Formosa had been responsible for the weakness of Japanese air power, and the accelerated assault on Leyte caught the Japanese air forces at their lowest ebb. If the original timetable for that assault (20 December) had been stickily maintained, Ozawa would have had new air groups trained, and the Japanese Navy could have put up a far better fight.

II

The Final Offensive

Only three weeks before this great naval battle, on 4 October 1944, the Joint Chiefs of Staff decided on the next move, to liberate Luzon and Manila, as General MacArthur had always wanted. Formosa was rejected in favor of Luzon on practical grounds. Despite Japanese occupation of the coast of China the Navy was still keen to take Formosa, because it would "put the cork in the bottle" of the South China Sea, complete the blockade of Japan, and provide an advanced air and naval base for the final assault. But the Army estimated that at least nine divisions would be required to take even a part of Formosa; and, owing to its deployment in Europe, nine divisions could not even be promised for the Pacific until June 1945. In the meantime, if the Leyte landing went well, the five divisions there employed and in reserve would be ready for a second major amphibious operation before the end of 1944; and five divisions would be enough to invade Luzon. Consequently, the landings at Lingayen Bay were put on the program for the end of December.

Admiral Nimitz was directed to start climbing the Bonins' ladder to Iwo Jima on 20 January 1945, and to prepare to occupy Okinawa or some other island in the Ryukyus on 1 March 1945. Iwo Jima was wanted as a staging and fueling point for B-29s engaged in bombing Japan from bases in the Marianas; Okinawa was a substitute for Formosa, or the China Coast, as the last stop before Japan.

The landings at Lingayen in Northern Luzon, postponed a couple of weeks, took place in January 1945, and although violently opposed by the new Japanese suicide or Kamikaze air tactics, were successful. While MacArthur's forces were battling for Manila, which fell on 25 February, Admiral Dan Barbey, the Seventh Fleet amphibious commander, planned operations to liberate Negros, Cebu, Mindanao and the other Philippine Islands.

According to plan, the Pacific Fleet under Nimitz conducted the amphibious operations against Iwo Jima and Okinawa. Both were prolonged beyond expectation by the Japanese tactics of digging into the limestone, or volcanic rock, and resisting to the last man. Iwo Jima was in the bag by April 1945, and Okinawa, invaded at Eastertime, held out stubbornly until July 1945. In taking Okinawa we were assisted by a British carrier group, which operated off the Sakashima Gunto and kept the Japanese suicide planes based on Formosa off our necks.

The first atomic bombs were dropped on Hiroshima and Nagasaki in August; Russia then belatedly declared war on Japan. The peace party in Japan induced the Emperor to surrender, after assurance from President Roosevelt and Mr. Churchill that the Allies had no intention of dictating to the Japanese their future form of government.

12

Atomic Bomb or Invasion of Japan?

We may well speculate what would have happened if we had not dropped those atomic bombs. If the war with Japan had not ended in the summer of 1945, the Allies would have invaded the southernmost Japanese island, Kyushu, that autumn, and Honshu, the central island where Tokyo is located, in January 1946. It has been estimated that those two operations, against die-hard, no-surrender Japanese, employing several thousand aircraft in suicide Kamikaze tactics, would have cost the Allies a million casualties. On the other hand, the submarines of the United States Navy had already worked around into the East China Sea and the Sea of Japan, cutting Japan itself completely off from her usual sources of food and fuel supply. Thus, the maritime blockade was almost complete, and it was only a matter of time before Japan was strangled and her principal cities destroyed by air bombing and naval bombardment.

Certain Japanese gentlemen with whom I have talked tell me that dropping the atomic bomb was a good thing; nothing less could have induced the Japanese Army chiefs to consent to an unconditional surrender. Others, who were in the peace party, believe that they could have persuaded the Emperor to surrender within a month, even if the atomic bomb had not been dropped. I do not know who was right; nobody knows or probably ever will know.

One thing, however, we can say for certain: that the United States Department of State and the British Foreign Office were absolutely right in assuring the Japanese they could keep the Emperor on his throne. That was a high strategic decision of great importance. There was strong left-wing pressure on our respective governments to depose the Emperor, on the false ground that he was the Japanese Hitler. Actually, Hirohito had never wanted war; he was forced into it by the military. The real force behind the demand for deposing the Emperor was Russia; Stalin hoped to throw Japan into anarchy, so that the Reds could establish a Communist dictatorship. It was Hirohito who issued the orders to surrender, and his subjects obeyed; we owe it to his character, as well as to General MacArthur's, that the Anglo-American occupation of Japan was the most peaceful, the most orderly, and (as we believe) the most beneficial in modern history.

Apart from the humanitarian arguments, which must be taken into account, against *using* the atomic bomb, was it not the *possession* of atomic weapons that contributed to the international tensions following the war? Can it be imagined that Russia would not have worked feverishly on nuclear development if we had simply tested the atomic bomb and not used it?

On the other hand, it was probably unfortunate that the war in the Pacific ended so abruptly. Had it lasted two or three months longer, proper preparations could have been made for the surrender of the Japanese armies in China. As it happened, the Communists profited by the confusion in China, and obtained most of the surrendered Japanese war materials. A slight prolongation of the war, moreover, would have enabled General MacArthur to carry out an operation that he had planned, to liberate the Dutch East Indies; and one can well imagine how much better it could have been for us — and, as I believe, for the Indonesians themselves — if an Allied army had been in Indonesia when the war ended.

13

Conclusion

Thus, the war in the Pacific was brilliantly concluded, in 1945 — far earlier than anyone in 1942 had supposed. When I talked with General MacArthur at Brisbane in 1943 he predicted that it would take many years to defeat Japan — actually it took a little more than two years from that time. At the Quebec Conference of September 1944, the Joint Chiefs of Staff argued that it would take only a year after the defeat of Germany to procure the unconditional surrender of Japan. The British Chiefs of Staff argued that it would take two years; so the C.C.S. compromised on a prediction of eighteen months. Actually it took only a little more than three months — 8 May to 11 August. And this was accomplished with far fewer American forces than were employed to help Britain and Russia defeat Germany. How did this happen?

First, by stupid strategy on the part of the Japanese — the Pearl Harbor attack, "Victory Disease," and their complete lack of knowledge or interest in defensive strategy.

Second, by the excessive Japanese inferiority in war production.

Third, by intelligent strategic planning on the part of Admiral King, Admiral Nimitz, General MacArthur and their staffs, as coördinated by the Joint Chiefs of Staff. After the initial defeats at Pearl Harbor, Wake Island, and the Philippines, they did not make a single major strategic error.

Fourth, by the superb fighting qualities of the American and Australian soldiers, marines, bluejackets and aviators.

In the Pacific the Allies started from scratch, with very low morale, to fight the supposedly invincible "Sons of Heaven"; but the United States Marines at Guadalcanal demonstrated that, man for man, they were the better fighters of the two; just as the naval aviators at the Battle of Midway, flying planes that were inferior to those of the Japanese, demonstrated their tactical superiority. In the Pacific, Guadalcanal and Midway had a moral and material effect similar to that of the Battle of El Alamein in the Mediterranean, or the turning of the tide against the U-boats in April 1943. Although the strategy that won the Pacific war was very largely American, the forces that implemented the strategy were not completely so. Australia and New Zealand contributed substantial naval and air forces. Australian divisions fought like wildcats in New Guinea; the New Zealand corvettes kept the Japanese submarines down. In the Okinawa campaign, as we have seen, a British fast carrier force covered the Allied southern flank; and later, a bombardment force of the Royal Navy helped the United States Pacific Fleet to pound down some of the industrial cities of Japan. And if the war against Japan had lasted much longer, British reinforcements would have been greater.

The Alliance between Great Britain and the United States, forged in the fire of necessity, was the most successful Grand Alliance in history. And the way was not smooth; as Lord Alanbrooke has well said, we were too closely related to make coöperation easy; and as General Sir Frederick Morgan has remarked, we used the same language, but with different meanings. With the help of Russia, this Alliance defeated the two most powerful military nations that have sprung up in the last one hundred and fifty years. For more than ten years after World War II ended, this Alliance has kept the peace against pressure by the Communists to break it up. A dangerous lesion in this Alliance developed in 1956. It is not my business here and now to examine why this happened, or who was responsible. That lesion is now being healed, and by the time this book appears I hope we may say that the patient has fully recovered.

In conclusion, I say, Health and strength to all efforts to preserve this Grand Alliance, and Woe! Woe! to those who would breach it. For an alliance, and still more, a cordial understanding between a strong United States and a powerful British Commonwealth is the greatest if not the only guarantee of peace in the world today.